DEAR READER,

They (whoever the infamous "they" are) will tell you the third time's the charm. But those of you who have had the pleasure of reading the previous editions of **Prism: Your LGBT Guide To Comics** know how "charming" they were: chock-full of comics, features, interviews and artwork representing the work of LGBT creators and/or works on LGBT-related themes.

Still, we know you'll find this latest edition of Prism Comics a worthy successor to those previous issues, and more. Within these covers—starting with another wonderful Joe Phillips work—you'll find articles that look at the queer year in comics, the LGBT scene in Europe, and a few views through humorous eyes (both Queer and, well, queer).

You'll find interviews with creators whose work is defining and extending the LGBT presence in the medium, whether through their own identities or through their characters. Giving evidence to how "we are everywhere" in the comics field as much as in the world at large, you'll find these creators' work everywhere from mini-comics to the independent press to the Big Two. Among others, we're proud to give you

a chance to visit with Steve MacIsaac, the first recipient of a Prism Comics grant supporting his work.

The comics you'll find herein, too, run the gamut from the frivolous to the profound (and who's to say a piece can't be both?!), representing the same range of publishers, from self-published projects to one of the most interesting and challenging series to come out of the DC/Wildstorm auspices in years.

This year has brought a "perfect storm" of growing influence: greater presence of comics projects in mainstream media, greater presence of LGBT projects in the medium, and greater recognition of comics in the LGBT press. We're proud to play a part in that, and to bring you another cross-section of the LGBT year in comics.

And for me, what makes this issue "the charm" is simple: my lucky charm must be working, letting me go beyond my seat at your side as an enlightened and entertained reader of the first two issues to take this spot in the front of the GUIDE to welcome you.

Now join me, sit back, and prepare to be entertained, educated, and, well, charmed.

Roger B.A. Klorese
President, Prism Comics

features

interviews

CONTENTS

CONTENTS

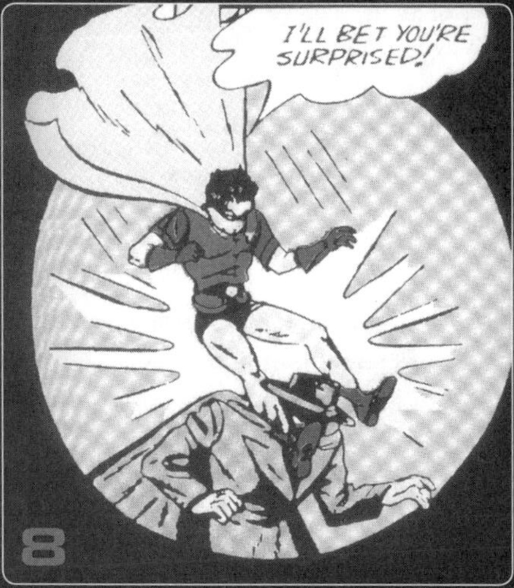

I'LL BET YOU'RE SURPRISED!

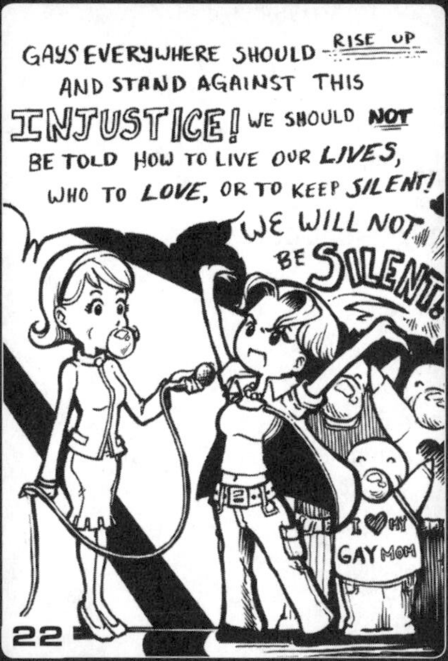

GAYS EVERYWHERE SHOULD RISE UP AND STAND AGAINST THIS INJUSTICE! WE SHOULD NOT BE TOLD HOW TO LIVE OUR LIVES, WHO TO LOVE, OR TO KEEP SILENT!
WE WILL NOT BE SILENT!
I ♥ MY GAY MOM

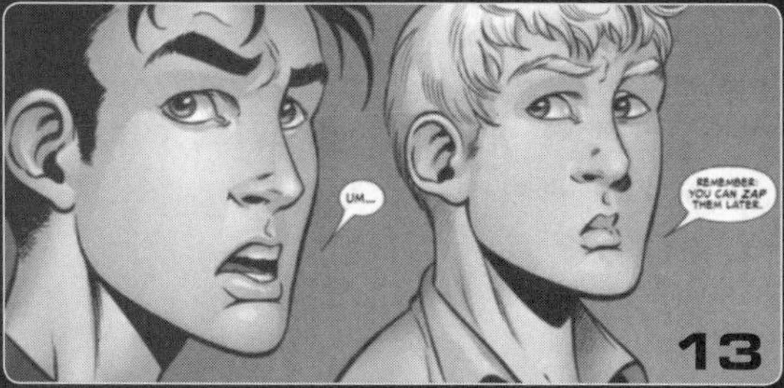

UM...
REMEMBER: YOU CAN ZAP THEM LATER.

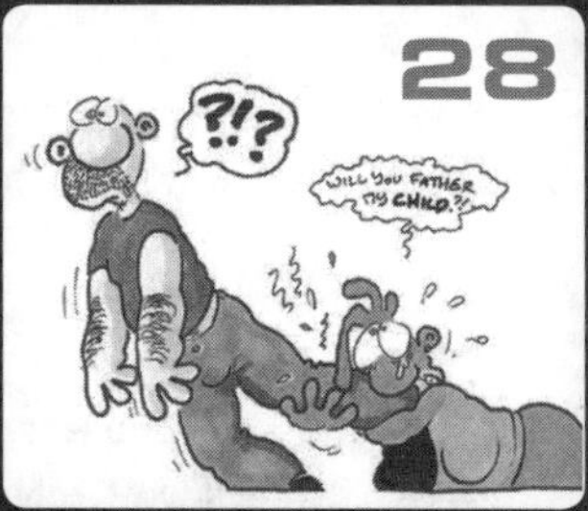

?!?
WILL YOU FATHER MY CHILD?!

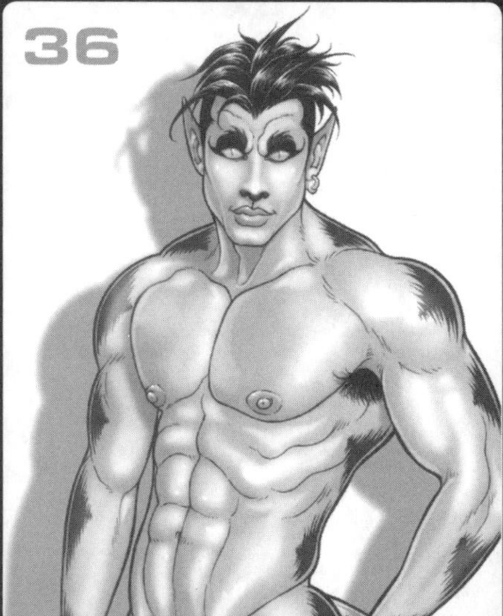

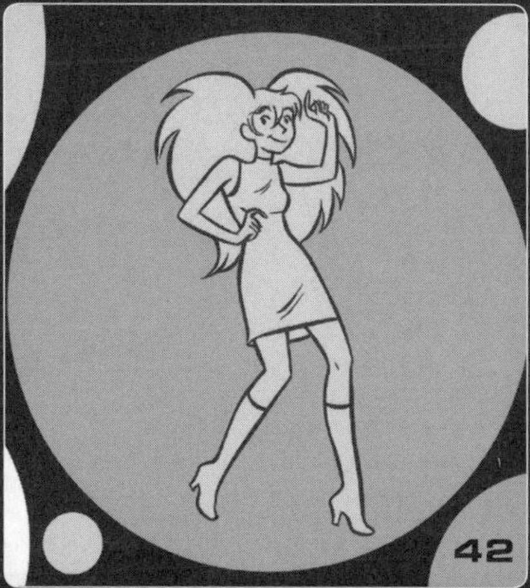

and then ......

CONTENTS

comics

Prism Comics: Your LGBT Guide to Comics #4, February 2006. Published annually by PRISM COMICS, a nonprofit organization promoting the work of lesbian, gay, bisexual and transgendered creators in comics, as well as LGBT issues in comics in general. Single issues: $5.95 U.S. All contents are © 2006 PRISM COMICS except where noted within. All artwork and covers have been presented and utilized for historical and review purposes only, and no infringement is intended or should be inferred. Permission to reprint portions of this publication, as well as advertising rates for future editions, may be requested through PRISM COMICS, 47 Lenox Pointe, NE, Atlanta, GA 30324, **www.prismcomics.org**. First printing. PRINTED IN USA. ISBN 0-9759164-1-6

CONTENTS

65

That's got to be your mother. And I thought she only interrupted us during sex.

88

73

BAM
BAM

76

SCREW THE POLLS.

94

ON THE COVER Heroes of indie, manga, and spandex unite in the cause of LGBT comics. Brought to you by artist JOE PHILLIPS.

CHILL DUDES, I GOT THIS ONE.

C R E D I T S

EDITOR SHAUN MANNING

DESIGNER ERIK BAXTER

CONTRIBUTORS
PAIGE AND KEVIN ALEXIS, SCOTT ANDERSON, RYAN BURTON, JUSTIN HALL, LYLE MASAKI, SEAN MCGRATH, RIVKAH, LAWRENCE SCHIMEL

BOARD OF DIRECTORS
ROGER B.A. KLORESE, PRESIDENT; MICHAEL LOVITZ, SECRETARY; MARCO MAGANA, TREASURER; TED ABENHEIM; CHARLES "ZAN" CHRISTENSEN; LINDA MAEPA; DAVID STANLEY; RICH THIGPEN

ADVISORY BOARD
PAIGE BRADDOCK, COLLEEN COOVER, TIM FISH, TERRANCE GRIEP, ANDY MANGELS, JOE PHILLIPS, JOSE VILLARRUBIA

to be continued next edition ......

CONTENTS

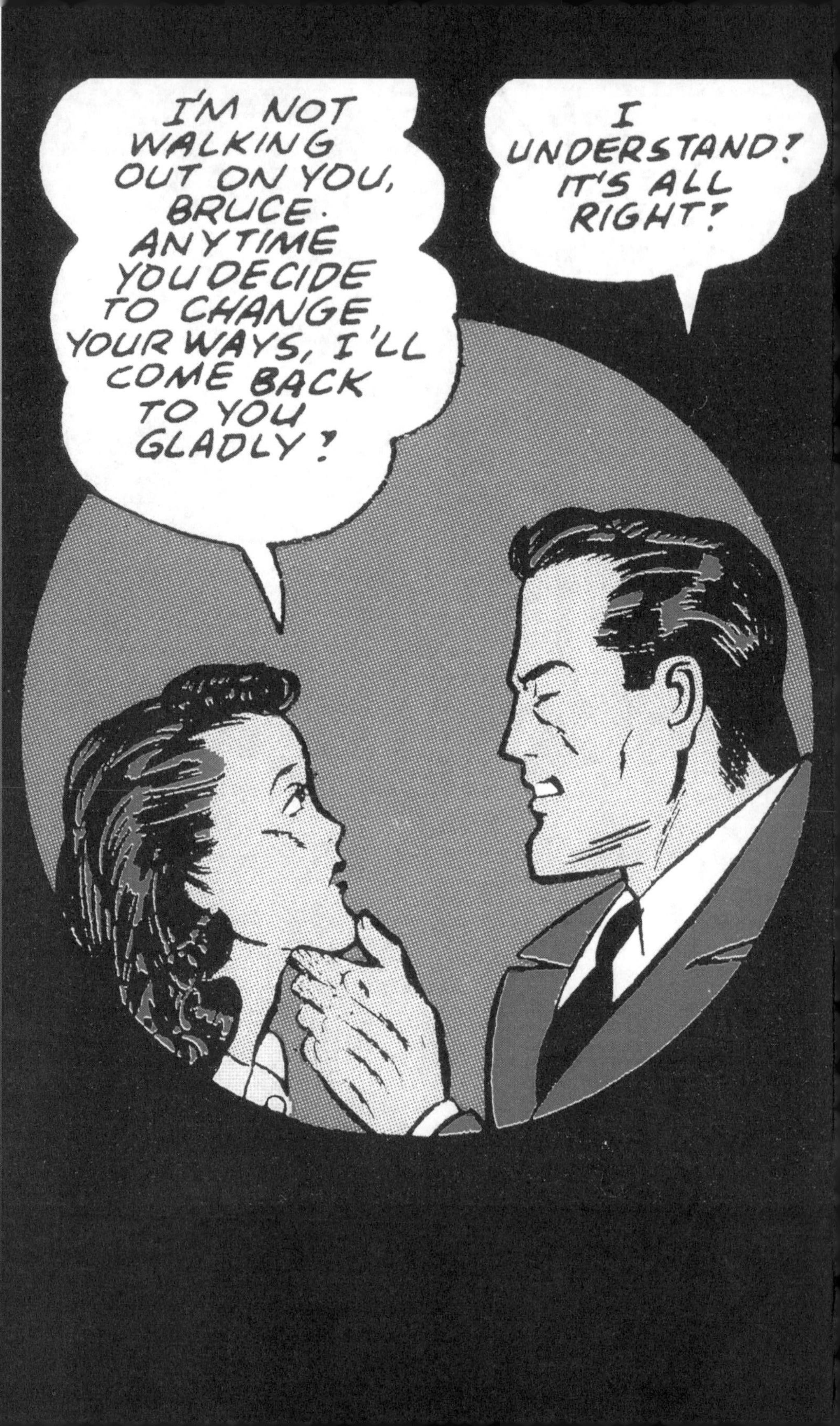
I'M NOT WALKING OUT ON YOU, BRUCE. ANYTIME YOU DECIDE TO CHANGE YOUR WAYS, I'LL COME BACK TO YOU GLADLY!
I UNDERSTAND! IT'S ALL RIGHT!

> Comic books, like other books, can be read at different levels, with different people getting out of them different things.

– Seduction of the Innocent
by Fredric Wertham (Rinehart & Company,
Inc. New York, Toronto 1953, 1954)

QUEER EYE ON COMICS SPECIAL:
BATMAN & ROBIN by Scott Anderson

When Prism Comics first announced that it was going to do a humor column called "Queer Eye on Comics," the announcement was met with disdain by some comic fans. "Do we really need more Batman and Robin jokes?" one critic asked, adding, "And were any of them ever funny in the first place?" Well, I was incensed! What would make this ninny think that we'd be doing Batman and Robin jokes? Years later, we still haven't. We'd have to be completely lacking in imagination to slip into something so very easy.

But boy oh boy, Batman and Robin are soooo gay. "How gay are they?" you ask. They're so gay their utility belts contain Astroglide and track lighting. They're so gay the original Bat-Signal was blaring the Funny Girl cast album. They're so gay that the Riddler could have discovered their secret identities from genetic samples they left at The Gotham City Baths if only he hadn't swallowed.

They're so gay ...

PRISM COMICS 7

...or are they?

Where did all these rumors of sodomy come from? Why are these two literally the poster boys for gay superheroes? Even in this day of out gay heroes, Batman and Robin still seem to evoke more speculation and tittering than a Tom Cruse marriage. But why them? Is it the Bat Poles? The gym bunny pecs? The overabundance of fashion accessories?

Well, yes, but more to the point it was Dr. Frederic Wertham, a psychiatrist who wrote in his book Seduction of the Innocent that comic books, specifically those with Batman and Robin and Wonder Woman, promoted homosexuality. Wertham wrote:

> Several years ago a California psychiatrist pointed out that the Batman stories are psychologically homosexual. Our researches confirm this entirely. Only someone ignorant of the fundamentals of psychiatry and of the psychopathology of sex can fail to realize a subtle atmosphere of homoerotism which pervades the adventures of the mature "Batman" and his young friend "Robin."

So there you have it. If you don't see just how faggy those two are, well, you're just ignorant. And Wertham's research was above reproach. For instance, he found some gay fellows who read Batman comics. Compelling evidence indeed! The good doctor also exposed the subtly queer undertones of the insidious comic.

It is like a wish dream of two homosexuals living together.

At home they lead an idyllic life. They are Bruce Wayne and "Dick" Grayson. Bruce Wayne is described as a "socialite" and the official relationship is that Dick is Bruce's ward. They live in sumptuous quarters, with beautiful flowers in large vases, and have a butler, Alfred. Batman is sometimes shown in a dressing gown. As they sit by the fireplace the young boy sometimes worries about his partner: "Something's wrong with Bruce. He hasn't been himself these past few days." It is like a wish dream of two homosexuals living together.

I can't argue with that. How I've dreamed of wondering what was wrong with my boyfriend. And sumptuous living? Hell, yeah! I like my beer cold, my TV loud, and vases large. Before I date a guy, I'll ask him how big his vase is, and I wear a pottery shard in the back left pocket of my jeans, so he'll know I'm serious. Wertham demonstrates Dick's sexual allure by writing, "He often stands with his legs spread, the genital region discreetly evident." Admittedly, "discreetly evident" is an oxymoron like "jumbo shrimp," "non-alcoholic beer," or "Fox News," but that this duo was gay is anything but ambiguous.

Or was Wertham a little off?

I recently bought the first BATMAN ARCHIVES (and at only $19.95, such a deal!), and I was surprised to see just how much heterosexuality was in those early classics. Oh, sure there are some suspiciously fey moments too, but for the most part, Bruce and Dick come off as breeders.

Despite the fact that Wertham tells us "In these stories there are practically no decent, attractive, successful women", the first suggestion of Batman's sexuality comes in DETECTIVE COMICS #31, where we meet Bruce Wayne's fiancée. You read that correctly. Fiancée. Unless you've read those Golden Age goodies, you probably didn't even know he had a fiancée, and if you were to guess her name, you'd probably say "Vicky Vale." At least, that's who I would have guessed was Batman's first love interest. But I'd have been wrong.

Her name was Julie Madison.

We meet the all but forgotten Ms. Madison as she walks the streets of Gotham in her off the shoulder robe with a flawless Marcel wave in her hair. She looks quite fetching even if she is hypnotized and trying to strangle a man. As it turns out, the Monk, a vampire with a penchant for wearing scarlet evening gowns and hoods, has put the whammy on Julie and is using her in his plot to … well, we never really learn what the Monk's plot was or why he'd chosen a whisper-thin, unarmed actress as his murderess, but that's not the point. The point is she looks fabulous throughout her adventures.

To get over her trauma of being a killer zombie, her doctor prescribes "an ocean voyage to Paris ... and perhaps, later, to Hungary – the land of history and <u>werewolves</u>." (Little known fact: for a brief few and unsuccessful years, the motto of the Hungary Board of Tourism was "Come for the history. Stay for the werewolves!") While we're left wondering if Julie's HMO will cover a bizarre curative that could only have been concocted by a graduate of the Dr. Frankenstein School of Medicine, our girl is unruffled in her pillbox hat with its jaunty bow. A quick, Cher-like change later and Julie is in a splendid green gown with white gloves and a matching feathered cap, boarding her cruise. Bow-tied Bruce is there to say goodbye. See? He must be straight. What gay man would follow around a gorgeous, yet mysteriously tragic, actress who frequently changes into ever more fabulous couture?

Hmm. OK, that sounds a little gay.

But when we see how devoted Batman is to her, we know it must be true, heterosexual love. No sooner has Julie left than he hops into his Batgyro (it's a combination airplane and helicopter, not a disgusting variation on the Greek sandwich) and flies out to meet her on the high seas. On the steamer, they are again attacked by the Monk, so Batman hightails it to his Batgyro and flies off to gay Paris, leaving his fiancé to the Monk's undead mercies. Admittedly, that does seem like he's less interested in her wellbeing than we'd expect from a heterosexual fiancée, but he does later scour Paris looking for her. When he spots a speeding car carrying Julie, he throws a sleeping gas pellet through a window, causing the car to crash into a tree. Yes, that does seem like a rather casual disregard for her safety, but he scoops her up, puts her in the Batgyro, and flies her to Hungary, the … umm … land of werewolves. Maybe not the best decision, but while in Hungary, he spies a racing carriage and inexplicable murders the driver by throwing him from the moving coach. He also tosses a sleeping gas pellet into the carriage and kidnaps a hooded female passenger, who he takes to Julie's hotel room. Why does he put this strange woman in his fiancée's room? Beats me, but the hooded woman is a vampire named Dala, who snacks on Julie's lovely neck while Batman waits outside. Batman recaptures Dala and decides to travel with her to the Monk's castle. To protect the tragedy-prone Julie, he hands her a stack of cash and says, "This money will safeguard you. I'm going."

I know what you're thinking, but just because Bruce Wayne shipped his fiancé off to the land of werewolves, caused her to be in a nasty car wreck, and thrice left to fend for herself against vampires while he gallivanted around town in a leather underpants is no reason to think he was subconsciously trying to off her so he won't have to marry her because he's gay. You can tell he's straight because after spending a night with Julie, he gives her a wad of money as if she were a hooker, just like *Pretty Woman* with Batman as Richard Gere. What could be straighter?

Oh, and the story ends with Batman battling werewolves and a giant gorilla before he hero-ically shoots the Monk and Dala in their sleep.

We see neither gown nor coif of Julie for several issues, but in DETECTIVE COMICS #38, Robin, the boy wonder, makes his debut. He's referred to as "The Sensational Character Find of 1940," as if they'd discovered him serving egg creams at Schwab's Drugstore. In two pages, Dick Grayson goes from member of a family trapeze act to orphan to elf-like sidekick and ward of a millionaire vigilante.

Dick doesn't get to live the glamorous jet set life for long. No sooner is he deemed ready for crime fighting than Bruce put him to work as "a grubby, dirty faced kid" hawking news-papers on the street. Of course, it's all so Dick can infiltrate the apparently lucrative news-boy protection racket. The blackmailing street toughs lead to Boss Zucco, the crime lord be-hind the murder of Dick's parents. With the

Robin's aerial acrobatics really come in handy... for cold-blooded murder

help of Dick's information, Batman is able to smash Zucco's gambling ring and then tricks Zucco and his band of thugs into trying to ambush him on the girder frame of a high-rise construction site. They are at least 9 stories off the ground, and there Robin's aerial acrobatics really come in handy… for cold-blooded murder. By my count, he causes at least three and as many as seven of Zucco's cronies to plunge to their deaths, smiling as he flips and kicks them to their doom. After Robin's killing spree, Batman shows up and dangles another thug by a rope around the thug's neck until the thug agrees to sign a confession. Zucco hears this, rushes forward, and shoves his squealing compatriot off the edge. The man screams in horror, silhouetted in moon light. Batman makes no move to save the man, but instead shouts, "Snap it, Robin!"

"Snap it?" I asked myself. What could it mean? Was Batman telling Robin to snap the Bat-Net tautly, so the plunging crook would be caught before splattering on the ground? Was it some 1940's lingo, telling Robin to "snap to it" and save the falling man?

Nope. It turns out that it was all a scheme to get Zucco to push the man from the building, so Robin could "snap" a photograph of Zucco in the act of killing him. "Got it!" Robin shouts glee-fully over the plunging man's screams. Apparently, Dr. Wertham should have worried less about the Dynamic Duo promoting homosexuality and more about them promoting snuff films.

Speaking of snuff films, two issues later Julie is back and making a horror film. In a scene where a character is supposed to be killed, the actress who plays her is actually murdered. When Julie confesses that she is terrified that she will be killed when she films her death scene the next day, Bruce, showing his typical concern for Julie's safety, says, "Don't worry dear. The murderer won't try for you." After Julie leaves, Bruce admits to Dick that he really does think she might be murdered. Feel the love. He barely saves Julie from the murderous Clayface, stopping the master of disguise in the act of throwing a dagger into Julie's back. Robin doesn't get to kill anyone in this issue. Still, he looks like he's having fun as he jumps, crotch first with this naked legs spread, onto Clayface's shoulders, shouting "I'll bet you're surprised!" Sorry, dear, but no. Dr. Wertham warned us all about you.

Julie again disappears for several issues as Bruce spends virtually all his time with his half-naked ward, but in issue #48, another woman enters Bruce's life. She's Linda Lewis, a torch singer who Bruce tries to pick up in a swanky nightclub. Why is Bruce trying to pick up Linda when he's engaged to Julie? Is he just that heterosexual? Is he trying to enhance his playboy image so no one suspects he's really Batman? Or is it symbolic of Wertham's Bat-Queen trying to schmooze with an up and coming Bette Midler? You, gentle reader, must decide for yourself because Bruce never gets his date. Before they can hook up, Linda Lewis is tricked into thinking she killed a man. Even after the mystery is cleared up, Bruce never pursues Linda Lewis again. Was it because gay Bruce was never interested in the first place? Was it because straight Bruce wouldn't date a ditzy blonde who could be tricked into thinking she killed a man? Or was it that he took one look at her initials and realized she'd stumbled into the wrong book and was supposed to be Superman? We can guess what Wertham would conclude, but if you're reading this, you probably know who Lori Lemaris is and the truth.

In the next issue, Clayface and, more importantly, Julie Madison are back. Moreover, we learn Julie and her horror film were a great success! So great that the studio has decided to give her a more glamorous name, one more fitting a starlet.

"She took the public by storm, and…" the head of the studio says.
His publicity man, Gabby, jumps in, "Storm. That's it! –But let's spell it S-T-O-R-M-E!"
"Storme – Not bad. Now a first name."
Gabby suggests, "Portia? Shakespeare's Portia! How do you like this? Portia Storme!"
"It's a natural!" the studio head agrees.
"Call up the newspapers, the movie mags to spread that name from here to Timbuctoo!"

Beside the unfortunate misspelling of Timbuktu, as I read that scene and considered the ill-fated Arnold Dorsey who got stuck with the stage name Engelbert Humperdinck, I couldn't help to think that the scene could have gone even more horribly wrong. In my mind, it went like this:

"Her name is too plain, Gabby," the studio head says. "But you should have heard the audience clap and …"
"Clap! That's it! But let's spell it C-L-A-P-P!"
"Clapp – Not bad. Now for a first name."
"Goneril? Shakespeare's Goneril! How do you like this? Goneril Clapp!"
"It's a natural! Call up the newspapers, the movie mags to spread Goneril Clapp from here to Timbuctoo!"

While Julie's life didn't go that far awry, she does break up with Bruce. Now a star on the rise, she feels that she can't be involved with someone as frivolous as Bruce. Bruce hardly seems broken up by this, perhaps confirming Wertham's hypothesis, and tells the newly dubbed Portia Storme, "In case you ever need me for anything, just holler. If ever there's anything I can do …"

"Thank you, Bruce," Portia interrupts, "but I don't think I'll ever be in much trouble."

Oh, snap! Coming from a woman who has been attacked by homicidal maniacs and vampires, saying that she doesn't think she could ever be in enough trouble to use his help is ice cold! A total Bette Davis style bitch. God, I love her, and I can see why a gay man would follow such an icon even to the land of werewolves. Maybe Wertham was on to something.

Alas, Portia does get into trouble when Clayface escapes from prison, bent on revenge! He heads directly to the studio and uses his knack for disguise to causes all sorts of mischief, not the least of which is leaving an unconscious Robin in the middle of a burning soundstage. When Batman sees what's going on, he douses himself with water and rushes toward the flames. When a firefighter tries to stop him, Batman says, "Listen, the best friend I've got lies in there – get out of my way!" He shoves the fireman and screams, "I'M GOING IN!" We see him braving the inferno, swinging through the smoke and unbearable heat. Flames licking at him, he drops into the very midst of the fire. Finally, with the burning set crumbling about him, Batman emerges with this youthful pal cradled in his arms. Had it been Julie in the fire, we can imagine him tossing her some cash and flitting away in the Batgyro.

What follows is a scene that would certainly have alarmed Dr. Wertham. Turning the tables on Clayface, Batman devises a plot to use disguises against him. To keep Clayface from murdering Julie, she disguises herself as Robin, and Robin disguises himself as Julie. Yes, Robin literally takes the place of Batman's love interest. Perhaps not coincidentally, this is the last issue in which Julie appears.

As she gazes at the man she'll never have, she says of Batman, "That's the sort of career I wish Bruce would pick for himself! But I guess that's wishing for the impossible!" One has to wonder with Dr. Wertham if Julie was willing to marry a man like Batman, if she'd shown she could handle herself with vampires and killers, why didn't Bruce tell her who he was instead of leaving her for the company of a young man? Why did he reveal his secrets to Dick on the very night he met him while hiding his double life from his fiancé at the expense of her love?

Is it because Batman is gay? Perhaps. Or perhaps it was sexism that kept the writers from considering Julie as a fellow crime fighter. Or perhaps Batman comics were a bit of entertaining fluff that shouldn't be overanalyzed.

That I and my fellow Queer Eye on Comics columnists poke fun at possible homosexual undertones in comics is understandable. We're joking around and we're gay. We should be looking for something of ourselves in comics. But when someone like Dr. Wertham rants about the dangers of gay images in comics, we have to wonder if he is "ignorant of the fundamentals of psychiatry." Has he heard of projection, where one sees in others what one fears in one's self? What would he think of the study that found that the men most opposed to homosexuality were the ones most aroused by gay porn? Would he examine the reasons he chose to work with troubled and homosexual young fellows with the same vigor that he examined Batman and Robin?

And so to the critics of Queer Eye on Comics, I say, yes, we do need more Batman and Robin jokes. (They're so gay the real reason they wear masks is to hide their oatmeal and eucalyptus exfoliating night cream and Liza eyelashes.) What we don't need are self-appointed guardians of our safety telling us what not to read. As Goneril Clapp might say, "Thank you, but I don't think we'll ever be in that much trouble."

2005

QUEER YEAR IN REVIEW

by

PKA

In a year dominated by giant comic book events promising to change the very landscape of mainstream comics, it's hard not to get lost in the frenzy of things. So this year it's more important than ever that we take a look back at everything, no matter how minuscule the queer content may be, so all is not overshadowed and forgotten.

Alpha Flight

▼ ▼ ▼ ▼ ▼

This year we got to see a glance of Northstar just before the third incarnation of ALPHA FLIGHT ended this past spring. Unfortunately, he didn't play a big role in the revival; in fact, he only had one line in all twelve issues. This title was satirical and somewhat untrue to its roots, but this was only disappointing if you were counting on what should have been guaranteed gay content. ALPHA FLIGHT did present us with the first gay mutant after all. The story, however, didn't seem to purposely push Norhtstar out of sight; the "all new, all different" Alpha Flight's big mission was to find out what happened to the original team.

The Authority: Revolution ▼ ▼ ▼ ▼ ▼

The Authority is a team of super powered individuals who got their start in a title called STORMWATCH. Since branching off on their own, THE AUTHORITY comics have made a lot of history with two of their members, Apollo and Midnighter who are openly gay, married and with adoptive child. With such an established couple, and a powerful one at that, you'd think there would be more queer content in the REVOLUTION series. The most the title gave us was a couple of kisses and a slew of slurs. Midnighter actually ends up leaving Apollo (and the team for that matter) midway through the series.

In this title, the team is now in the White House playing President and staff when Midnighter gets a message from a future Apollo warning him of the fate that awaits them if the team stays together. Midnighter eventually takes the advice and splits up the team. leaving Apollo to raise their daughter alone for three years. Slurs are one thing but when you split up the most noteworthy gay couple in comics it's a sad, sad day. Apollo doesn't even seem too upset about it, and in the last few issues when Midnighter does return, the characters still don't even seem bitter about how events had fallen between them.

It would appear that this go around, the REVOLUTION series failed to make another monumental step with its gay couple, rather taking a step back and forcing readers to accept that this title was too good to be true.

Catwoman

This year in CATWOMAN, we didn't see much of her out best friend Holly and Holly's girlfriend Karon. Though Catwoman often spoke to Holly via communicator, the character appeared only rarely, and Karon was even more scarcely seen. This is disappointing, but at least their relationship didn't take a turn for the worse, better known as cliche! There were no hate crimes surrounding the two or any slurs targeted at them—well, not unless you count a sly remark about the two from Scarface a slur. Then again, being called kinky can be taken as a compliment by some.

Either way, the only thing this comic had going for it this year community-wise was acceptance, which has pretty much been there since Holly's first appearance in the title. Having acceptance of a same sex couple in a title can go along way, but a little more visibility would have been nice.

Ex Machina

Issues 5-10 of the series dealt mainly with a strange alien symbol that kept showing up in New York city subways, and the deaths that seemed to be connected with its appearance. The F.B.I. contacts Mayor Hundred, an ex-super hero, because the person suspected to be responsible was a close friend of his. This same friend helped him a long time ago with interpretating what seems to be the same symbol, but that connection is one made by the reader and isn't really discussed. When Mayor Hundred requests to personally check things out, the F.B.I. agent tells him to focus on the gay marriage issue because her and her girlfriend would appreciate it. Early on in the arc, Hundred's deputy mayor Wylie explains that his brother Todd, a firefighter, and Todd's partner Bill, a Log Cabin Republican, wish to get married. This opens up serious debate for the issues to come. Mayor Hundred is determined to get these two married (despite being questioned here and there about his own sexuality) not only because he sees nothing wrong with marrying the two men but also because he made a promise to the fire department that he'd help them with whatever they needed. Hundred was even shot with an arrow at a press conference after expressing his views on marriage in general and what laws should be held in place to sanction it. This sounds like it should have a higher rating, but the truth of the matter is that the subject is still just an background story.

Gotham Central

This title really made an impact with readers in 2003 with the outing of Detective Renee Montoya in the arc, "Half a Life." In 2004, she just sort of slipped under the radar and was kept on the backburner, so we weren't really expecting a whole lot for 2005—but, surprisingly, this title delivered. Comics have a tendency, especially in the mainstream, to out a character and then either drop them completely or sweep them offstage, keeping them hidden and forgettable. GOTHAM CENTRAL did exactly the opposite.

In 2005, Renee's story comes full circle and the character begins a slow reconciliation with her father who disowned her after she admitted her homosexuality. For the most part her colleagues seem to be very cool with it but there is the occasional slur thrown at her from time to time. Best of all, Renee seems to be in a very happy and healthy relationship with her girlfriend, which is also something that isn't often seen in mainstream comics with queer characters. The title is very realistic and depicts Renee Montoya as a hard working detective who isn't afraid to take matters into her own hands, as shown in the arc "Keystone Kops," in which she squares off with Dr. Alchemy after he accuses her of beating her girlfriend.

We were really impressed with GOTHAM CENTRAL this year and hope to see more things like this in 2006.

GLA - Great Lakes Avengers

Now this little four-issue mini was some funny stuff, so if you're looking for laughs go no further—but if you're looking for some good quality GLBT material, keep walking. To be fair, GREAT LAKES AVENGERS actually had a pretty interesting story, and though the characters had some strange and to some extent mediocre powers they still managed to triumph at the end. These four issues weren't exactly littered with gay content, but even from the first issue you knew there was going to be some.

Take issue two for instance. There is a slight mix up when Flatman, "the 2-D defender" tries to recruit new members into the GLA. New recruit Living Lightening is very surprised to learn that what he thought was the Gay/Lesbian Alliance is actually a team called the Great Lake Avengers, and awkwardly zips off. This incident is later discovered, in the last issue, to inspire Flatman to come out.

On one hand it is really awesome that Flatman's teammate Doorman (a living portal), is so accepting and even proud of his friend for coming out. On the other hand, though, it seems to go almost unnoticed by the rest of the team because there are so many other events happening with some of the other characters that the outing unfortunately gets lost.

Mystique

We are so very disappointed to give this title such a low rating. Mystique has always been one to blur gender lines, and her comics convey extremely well how confident she is in both gender roles. The series started off really strong with lots of good hints about Mystique's bisexuality and even had a few drops about Destiny, a former love interest, but the series ended in a weirdly awful sort of way. The title even presented an issue early on with a transgendered thief that Mystique took pity on and ended up helping out by "financing" the thief's gender reassignment procedure. These earlier comics are an excellent read and shouldn't be passed up, but this is Queer Year in Review, after all, so we must focus on what's at hand for 2005, which is the last four issues of the series. The book ended earlier this year and unfortunately failed to deliver what readers thought early on in series to be a gay couple.

The series began with the death of Prudence Leighton, one of Xavier's agents who has the ability to inhabit the bodies of females. She is killed by a man named Steinbeck who has pyrokenetic abilities. It is after her death that Xavier asks Mystique to fill in as his spy. She accepts only because he promises to use some of Forge's technology to help her evade the authorities, who are trying to track her down. Not long into the series, Mystique meets a man named Shepard who asks her to play double agent. You soon find out Shepard is working for a man who he often refers to as "beloved." Mystique catches on to Shepard and does a little digging. She discovers that Shepard's real name is Francis Leighton, brother of Prudence Leighton, who has somehow possessed Steinbeck's body. This is who Shepard had been calling "beloved" to all this time. Yikes! So what was hoped to be a gay relationship actually turned out to be incestuous.

This series had a lot of twists and turns, and although close doesn't always cut it, Shepard was still willing to spend the rest of his life with another man, even if that man was inhabited by his sister. Readers can take from this what they will.

Runaways

This title really impressed us because it showed the confusion often felt when trying to come to terms with one's preference. There aren't exactly many hints or indications of how Karolina feels for her teammate Nico until the end of issue seven and all of issue eight. The two are walking from the store and they see a shooting star. Karolina, making a move, leans in to kiss Nico, but Nico backs away. Karolina immediately apologizes asking if she's moving too fast and Nico is unsure what to say because she didn't know Karolina liked girls. Nico questions her about it of course, not so much in a disgusted way but in a tone that makes Karolina have a shamed look as she tries to explain herself. She doesn't get too far in her explanation when a ship lands in front of them. As things would turn out, Karolina's evil parents promised her in marriage to a Skrull before they died. What was really great to see was that after Karolina tells the Skrull she can not marry him because she likes girls, the Skrull quickly and willingly changes into a female to suit her, since gender and preference really aren't issues for the Skrulls. Now not having any excuses she is forced to leave with the Skrull, but before she does she hands Nico the bracelet that keeps her powers at bay. She tells Nico that now she can finally stop hiding who she is. While the comment is probably meant about Karolina's true alien origin it really transcends boundaries, which is something very relatable to us all.

Ultimate X-Men

The chances of there being another gay mutant are becoming more colossal as hints are dropping more steadily in ULTIMATE X-MEN. So far UXM is proving to be very promising in the direction it seems to be going. In fact, speculation about Colossus' homosexuality has been an underlying story throughout the series and though hints may be getting tired it's still nice to see something present in one of Marvel's flagship titles. If for nothing else it at least shows some bit of hope.

While there is no serious gay content, Northstar has made several appearances. Not only did he come out [again] in issue 46 but he seems to be quite flirty with Colossus and doesn't seem to be the least bit shy about who he is. Northstar hasn't really been given a strong hold in the series thus far but it's nice to see his character being represented so well and true. The rating mostly reflects our feelings about Northstar's portrayal in UXM; it's probably the best you'll see of him this year. [Editor's note: As the Prism Guide was going to press, Colossus officially came out in ULTIMATE X-MEN #65. He will be going to prom with Northstar.]

Also surrounding the title was a little bit of an uproar with Longshot. Readers didn't seem hesitant when speculating about his homosexuality, but one should remember that Longshot was in a relationship with Spiral, a romance that ended with him killing the human she was seeing behind his back. In fact, the only reason why the X-Men came to Krakoa (the island where mutant criminals of Genosha are hunted for sport) was to investigate if he really committed the crime. Though Longshot did spend quite a lot of time with Colossus and the two did discuss fashion tips, we don't necessarily think he's gay, just maybe metrosexual. This may explain Spiral's fabulous new make over.

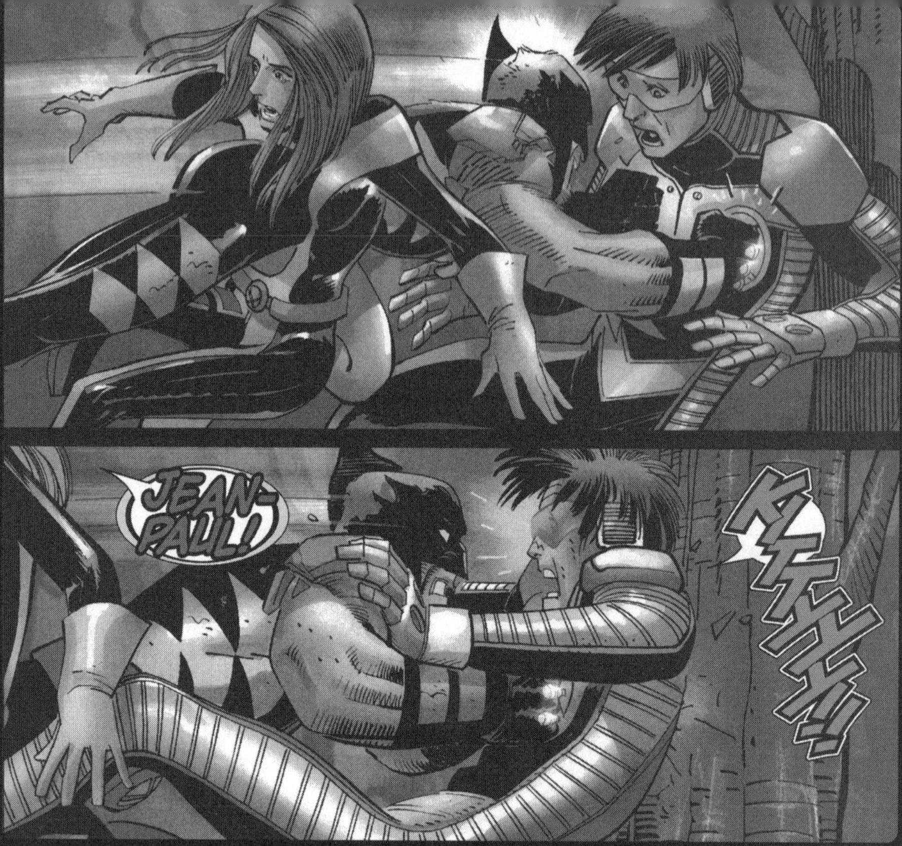
JEAN-PAUL!

Wolverine

In 2004's "Queer Year in Review", the question was asked "where is Jean-Paul?". We found him for the third and final time this year being killed and brought back to life in Wolverine: Enemy of the State (WOLVERINE 20-25) and Wolverine: Agent of S.H.E.I.L.D. (26-31). It wasn't pretty. At the end of issue 25, the openly gay mutant known as Northstar falls at the claws of Wolverine, who is under the control of HYDRA and The Hand. In the very next issue Northstar's remains are kidnapped and resurrected by The Hand who return him as an evil operative for the organization.

There was a ton of stuff happening in these twelve issues, including cameos of nearly every major Marvel character this side of Galactus, and though the two arcs were action packed it seemed more like a testosterone trip than a well thought out story. As much as we would have loved it to be, this was nothing to write home about. Northstar did not represent the community very well at all with his random killing sprees and his filler appearances.

Young Avengers ▼▼▼▼▼

YOUNG AVENGERS is one of those very rare titles that makes a lasting impression. We honestly weren't expecting much from this comic because we were too busy judging this book by its cover. So far, this title has a really well thought out and original story with a really nice set of characters. What amazed us though was that the title didn't try and hide its two young gay characters, who came out shortly into the series.

In issue 7, Billy (who is at this time known as Asgardian but will later go by Wiccan) with Ted (Hulkling) by his side tries to tell his parents that he's got super powers. Before he can say anything his parents are welcoming them both with open arms saying how proud they are of him [for trying to come out] and that they love him and are happy that they found each other. Now when does that ever happen in mainstream comics? That was just something so wonderful to read. It really sends a positive message, especially since the rest of the team seems to be perfectly fine with the young gay couple, as well.

Also, something nice to note is that teammate Stature (Ant-man's daughter) makes the comment that no matter what happens, Wiccan and Hulkling will always have each other. Hopefully that holds true for 2006.

2005 may have brought some big changes but rarely were they seen pertaining to mainstream comics with any gay content, but give it time. Some say there is a considerable lack of gay characters in mainstream comics, but while the progress of inclusion has been painfully slow, our take on the matter is that there are plenty of gay characters in main-

> I came out to my dad at sixteen.

COMING OUT STRAIGHT

BY RIVKAH

I'M STANDING AT THE CAPITAL TODAY WHERE GAY TEENS HAVE GATHERED TO PROTEST HOUSE BILL #284~

RIVKAH GREULICH IS ONE.SUCH.TEEN.

I'd been wanting to tell him for weeks, but words aren't always so easy spoken aloud. My family was seated at the dinner table one night when I looked down at my plate, burst into tears, and refused to say another word. Food untouched, my father and I went for a walk while he played twenty questions:

"Did you fail a test?" A shake of the head, no.

"Are you having problems with your friends?" Another shake.

"Are you pregnant?" This time I shut my eyes and laugh a little. "Not unless I'm the Virgin Mary." He asks a few more fatherly-type questions—you know, the random ones only parents think to ask, usually involving drugs, sex, or love—until finally he stops and turns to me, "Do you think you're gay?" I hesitate a moment and then I look at him, and that was all he needed to know. He sat down and cried.

. . . .

I grew up in a loving but relatively conservative Christian family. My parents met at bible college, and I still vividly remember evening discussions in the car with my mother, headed to her house for the weekend while we discussed God, the bible, and faith—soft gold Texas summer grass blurring past my window as I contemplated her words, and she mine. We went to church on Sundays, and I went to youth group on Wednesdays. Acceptance of a lesbian daughter came neither quick nor easy for my father—a man who had believed his whole life that homosexuality was immoral and taught his children the same—but eventually, with time, understanding, and example (and a girlfriend over at Thanksgiving), he opened his eyes and finally saw his youngest daughter not as a lesbian, but as a woman, reconciling his faith with love and acceptance.

Our coming out stories are told not just by the gay men, lesbian women, bisexual, and transgender people of the world but also by the people we love and whom love us in return. Friends, family, and acquaintances alike. For many, it's a form of loss, grief, and denial. For some it's a source of pride. For others, it isn't even an issue—like telling a friend you prefer Canary yellow over Prussian blue.

The premise of my first graphic novel series, STEADY BEAT, is the story of teenaged Leah Winters who discovers a love letter addressed to her sister from another girl. There are questions, answers, fears, hopes, dreams, and finally . . . well, you're just going to have to read to find out. The situation is made complex due to the two girls being the daughters of a Texan Republican State Senator and the fact that Leah's sister, Sarai, is this supposed model of perfection to peers and family alike. STEADY BEAT shows the things we take for granted in other people and the result of suddenly seeing within them the unexpected and precious. It's not just one coming out story, but many. Of the mother, the sister, their friends, and their

community. It's an experiment in both perspective and format, constantly evolving as it progresses and unraveling through the eyes of one naïve and innocent and very straight girl.

When I sat down to write STEADY BEAT, it was not to write from my own viewpoint, but rather through the eyes of someone like my father. Someone who's never thought, "What if?" because it's never been an issue. If I were my sister, and she were coming out to me, how would I react? I spent hours in my car, listening to music and imaging myself as that character. Would Leah be accepting? Would she be angry? Would she grow through denial? How would her coming out story unfold?

It was an incredible struggle imagining myself in that position, someone who's always simply known that I'm gay (bisexual, really, but that's another story entirely). If someone comes out to me, I treat it like it's no big deal because I've been there. But what about those who haven't and never will? I have to constantly resist the urge to write from the vantage of the gay sister. That was an easier story for me because it

was my own, personal story, but STEADY BEAT is supposed to be something every teenager can relate to, not just gay teens.

At times I've succeed in my first attempts, and at times I've failed. STEADY BEAT doesn't read like most comics. It's a single, self-contained story spread out through several volumes. To an extent, I'd almost discourage reading the first volume until the rest are out! It's like picking up a novel and only reading it a quarter of the way through. You meet the characters and get the start of a plot, but there is neither climax nor conclusion due to the natural rhythm of the story, where climax and conclusion come at the middle and end, not the beginning. Considering the story is slated for 3 volumes (though I've written it for four), you can imagine exactly where middle and end fall. Volume 2 is due out Spring 2006, and since STEADY BEAT is sold in the same format as other Tokyopop graphic novels, it's typically found in the manga section of book and comic stores.

I will never forget the day I realized my father had told all of his coworkers and friends about his youngest daughter's girlfriend. Not because he was worried about who I was dating, but because he's proud of me. For my being active in the GLBT community. For the strength I've found to be incredibly open and never hide my orientation and my love. Proud I have no qualms about holding another girl's hand in public. Proud of me following my dreams ... of my writing this story.

This is partially my story. And it's partially his. Partially everybody's story. It's for those who've been me to realize they're not alone, and for those who've never been there to be given the chance to sit in my characters' heads and experience it for themselves.

My first graphic novel may be far from perfect (I'm really just getting started!) but it's written from the heart. By the time the full story has played out, I hope that Leah and Sarai Winters make a few people think and open a few minds in return. . . . .

Enjoy an excerpt from Rivkah's STEADY BEAT, Volume 1

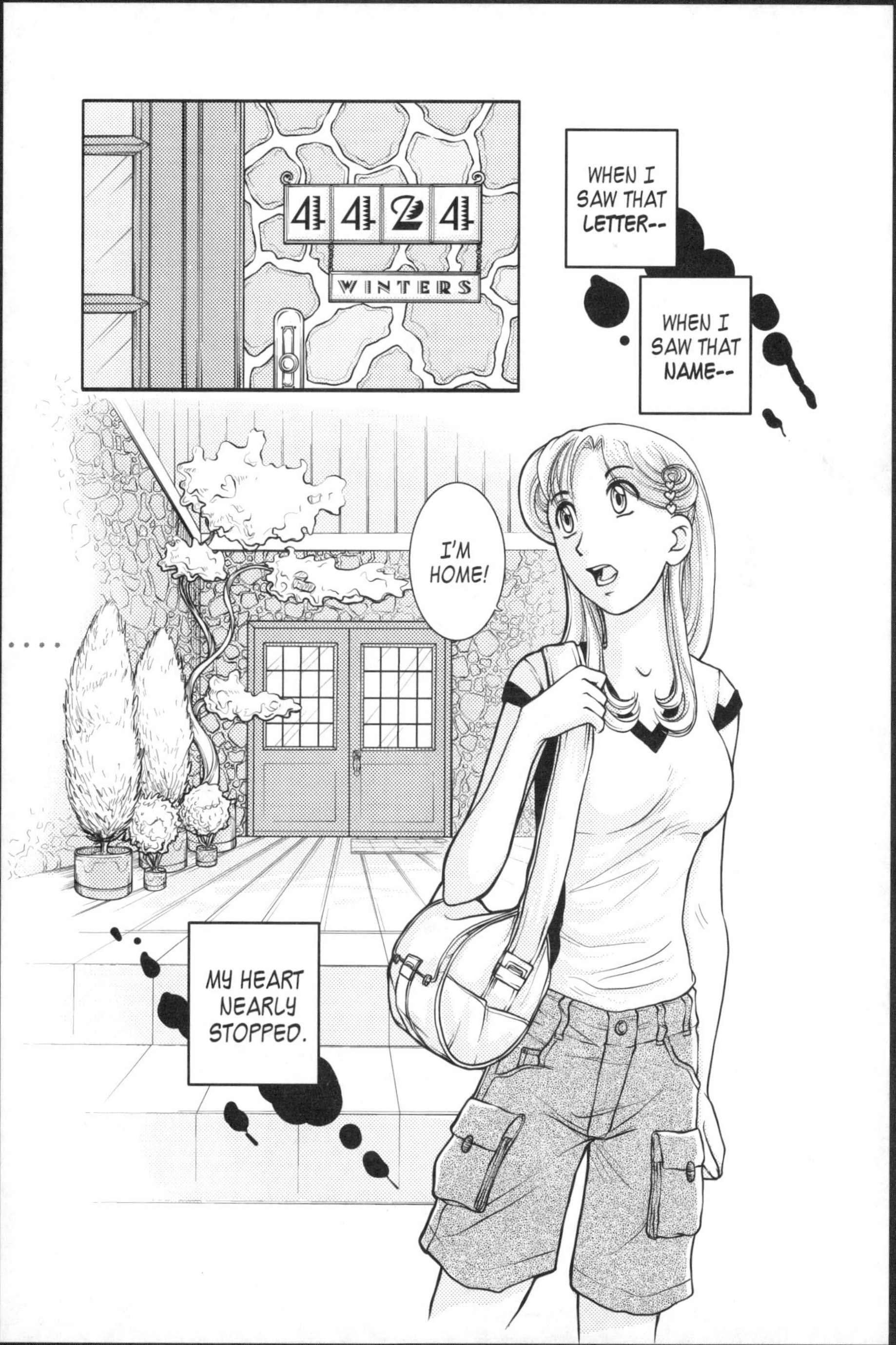
4424
WINTERS
WHEN I SAW THAT LETTER--
WHEN I SAW THAT NAME--
I'M HOME!
MY HEART NEARLY STOPPED.

Excerpt from *Steady Beat*, volume 1. © 2005 Rivkah and TOKYOPOP Inc.

SHE'D KILL ME!

AND SARAI'S BROUGHT BOY-FRIENDS HOME BEFORE.

I KNOW SHE'S BEEN ON **DATES** WITH THEM.

WHO KNOWS WHAT **ELSE** SHE'S DONE!!!

SHE IS 18!

I COULD BE WRONG.

Excerpt from *Steady Beat*, volume 1. © 2005 Rivkah and TOKYOPOP Inc.

european unions

by Lawrence Schimel

the
netherlands

germany

france

spain

Shortly after I moved to Europe seven years ago, I often heard the following joke: What do you call someone who speaks three languages? Trilingual. What do you call someone who speaks two languages? Bilingual. What do you call someone who speaks only one language? American.

Embarrassing as it might be to be the butt of such jokes, the truth of the matter is that the English-speaking world, in general, expresses little interest in the literatures of other languages and countries. According to UNESCO, while 50% of all translations around the world are from English, only 6% are translated into English. According to a recent NEA study, out of 10,000 works of poetry and fiction published in the U.S. that year, a mere 300 of said books were translations into English from another language.

Given the rich tradition of European comics, the percentage of translations for graphic novels is somewhat higher, but even still there are a vast many titles which are completely unknown in English.

This article does not pretend to be exhaustive, but rather to give a few brief highlights of the world of queer comics in other languages, which might not be familiar yet to Prism readers.

france

In 1994, **Fabrice Neaud** co-founded the publishing collective Ego comme X, which published a magazine of that same name as well as bringing out graphic novels. He began to publish an autobiography titled simply JOURNAL ("Diary"), first in the magazine and later as albums, of which 4 volumes have been published to date. His realistic black and white drawings, with their frank and often explicit depictions of gay life in a small town in France (in particular, Angouleme, home of the most famous European comics conventions each January) are an ambitious chronicle of desires fulfilled and frustrated, totaling approximately 800 pages so far.

French queer publisher H&O has been publishing a number of gay comics in translation (Tim Fish, Tom Bouden, etc.) and have also brought out an original hardcover volume, in French and English, of **Patrick Fillion**'s drawings titled BOYTOONS, as well as original erotic comics: RAINBOW COUNTRY by **Max and Porky** and LE PORNOMICON by **Logan**.

the netherlands

Tom Bouden is the best-known queer comics artist in the Netherlands, who ha regularly been publishing in numerous periodicals such as GAY KRANT, QUEER, and FRESHMEN, as well as having published over a dozen albums of his work,both through his own company and through other publishers. He was recently introduced to English-language readers by Green Candy Press, which brought out a collection of his comics about MAX & SVEN. Bouden's adaptation of Oscar Wilde's The Importance of Being Ernest was also published in English by German publisher Männerschwarmskript Verlag.

Floor de Goede is a young artist (25 as this is being written) who publishes a black and white strip featuring his alter ego, Flo, in the Dutch queer youth magazine Expreszo, as well as in a daily webcomic (www.doyouknowflo.com). The first compilation of the strip has been published by Belgian comics publisher Bries.

germany

Ralf König is, indisputably, one of the most popular and most prolific gay comics artists in the world. Curiously, while his work has been widely translated in other countries, there have been few English-language editions of his comix available: until now. Two of his regular publishers have decided to bring out English-language editions of some of his bestselling titles. German publisher Maennerschwarm Skript Verlag has brought out a translation of ROY & AL, a hilarious look at gay life from the point of view of two dogs (the Roy and Al of the title), one a mutt and the other purebred, who are thrown together when their owners hook up. Spanish publisher Ediciones la Cupula is bringing out a translation of WIE DIE KARNICKEL ("Like Rabbits"), contrasting the sexual and romantic relationship of two neighbors, one straight and one gay, and especially the differences in how each deals with the world of pornography and fantasy.

Three of König's comics have been adapted into films: ATTACK OF THE KILLER CONDOM, PRETTY BABY, and LYSISTRATA.

Berlin artist **Stefan Zeh** is a frequent contributor to German gay periodicals, and Heinz und Horst Verlag published a compilation of his dark and sardonic strips featuring leathermen Ben and Axel and their friends under the title KURZGESCHORN ("Close-cropped").

Cologne artist **Swen Marcel** has published two camp graphic novels featuring character David: DER SEXPERTENBERICHT, showcasing erotic escapades including a gangbang party, moonlight cruising, etc.; and LA FINCA, a romp through Ibiza featuring drag queens, masked criminals, and hunky boys. Both books are published by Mattei Medien.

page 15 of WIE DIE KARNICKEL
["Like Rabbits"]
Ralf König

Bruno Gmünder has recently branched out from publishing nude photobooks to aggressively try to corner the gay comics market, primarily through English-language editions for the world market, many of which also have smaller German-language editions as well. Starting with Joe Phillips, Bruno Gmünder Verlag GmbH has recently begun

page 20 of ROY & AL
Ralf König

publishing the much more explicit comics of Patrick Fillion. Other books include one-off titles like MANGA BOYS by Kinu Sekigushi or the recent compendium titled PRIME CUTS by Howard Strangroom and Stephen Lowther, collecting their strips from the 80s and 90s that first appeared in GAY COMIX, MEATMEN, and other venues.

spain

Nazario, granddaddy of queer comics in Spain, began publishing in the '70s in the first gay magazines emerging toward the end of the Franco dictatorship. Probably best-known for his perverse transsexual series ANARCOMA, published in English by Catalan Communication in 1983, he has recently published various retrospectives of his work, including PLAZA REAL: SAFARI.

Another recently-recovered classic of gay comics is the hardcover volume MANUEL NO ESTÁ SOLO ("Manuel is not alone") by **Rodrigo**, published by sins entido in 2005. It collects the wordless, black and white comic about Manuel and his infatuation and relationship with a hirsute man he meets at the pool, along with various other drawings and short strips published in magazine in the '80s, all of which realistically reflect Madrid of that epoch.

Queer Spanish publisher Editorial Egales was at the forefront of contemporary efforts in Spain to revitalize queer comix, bringing out the first two volumes of Alison Bechdel's DYKES TO WATCH OUT FOR (Ediciones La Cúpula is now also publishing the series, starting from the more recent volumes) and my own graphic novel, VACACIONES EN IBIZA (published in English by NBM).

Recently, comics publisher Ediciones La Cúpula (which has for many years enjoyed tremendous success with their Spanish translations of Ralf König) has decided to aggressively embrace the gay and lesbian comix world, with an imprint (indicated only by a small rainbow flag) featuring primarily translations of authors such as Tom Bouden, Paige Braddock, or Howard Cruse, plus a new magazine (only for boys) titled CLARO QUE SÍ ("But of Course") featuring a mix of international comics (Joe Phillips, CHELSEA BOYS, etc.) plus new Spanish creators as well.

Spain's new generation of creators

Probably best-known to English-speaking readers is **Ismael Álvarez**, a young artist best known for his erotic drawings, who has been illustrating some of Patrick Fillion's characters for Class Comics.

Author **Javi Cuho** and artist **David Cantero** have self-published the first volume of a manga-influenced black and white comic titled FALLEN AN-GELS (in Spanish despite the English title). The duo has a second volume in the works, among other projects. Cuho has also worked with other Spanish artists, such as **Hokane**, to produce the erotic title NO TE ESPE-RABA for Libido Ediciones.

HISTORIAS DE LOLA by the team ELENApuntoG, composed of the self-taught artist **Elena Guardia** and the author **María Ángeles Cabré**, is a collection of single-panel dyke toons featuring the eponymous character: Lola. Published in May 2005 by Ediciones La Tempestad, it is one of the rare lesbian incursions into the world of European comics.

La Tempestad also published two collective volumes of gay comics: HIS-TORÍAS DE CHICOS (Boy Tales) and HISTORÍAS DE STIGES (Sitges Tales), both now out of print.

Well-known throughout the Spanish-speaking world thanks to his dynamic website and long-running blog, not to mention his frequent contributions to numerous Spanish magazines including the recently-launched Claro Que Sí, Ismael Álvarez has recently come to the attention of the English-speaking world through his collaborations with Patrick Fillion. Lawrence Schimel has translated his responses to a few questions:

· ·

LAWRENCE SCHIMEL: How did you meet Patrick?

ISMAEL ÁLVAREZ: I still haven't had the pleasure of meeting Patrick in person. Everything happened over the internet. I had known of his work for a long time and decided to get in touch with him. Little by little, we began forming a strong friendship that has also developed into something more, professionally speaking.

LS: How did the idea of working together come up?

IA: It all began with some fan art that I drew for him as a gift. Patrick always liked my style of working, and he loved seeing his characters drawn by me and offered to work with me on various of his projects, such as RAPTURE. It seemed like a great idea to me, since I've admired his work for so long and it was an honor to work together with him.

LS: Is it harder to illustrate someone else's characters than your own?

IA: It's much more difficult, since you have to follow certain guidelines and make them seem as similar as possible. Although Patrick has always given me a lot of liberty and lets me draw them in my style without their losing one whit of their charisma.

taboo

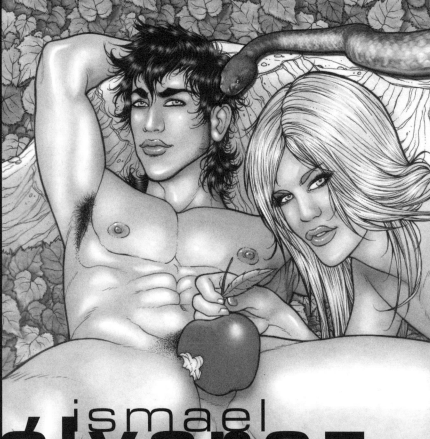

ismael
álvarez

by Lawrence Schimel

LS: What tools do you use when you work?

IA: Everything. Manual and digital. I mean that normally I use a mix of traditional and electronic steps, that is, I draw pencils and color by hand, scan, digitally retouch things with Photoshop or Painter, etc. It all depends on how I want the final image to look.

LS: How did you begin in the world of comics and illustrations?

IA: For as long as I can remember I've drawn, but professionally I've been taking part in this world since I was 17. Around then, I began publishing in various manga magazines, when the Nippon fever was just arriving in Spain. Later, I began to work with the publisher Megamultimedia, for their erotic magazines like Hentaiwet and Wetxomic. From there, I also began to work with many foreign publishers as well, for magazines, posters, calenders, etc.

LS: Do you feel any shame at being so well- known for such explicit drawings?

IA: Not at all, I love drawing erotic comics and illustration, and I will keep doing it. For many people, sex is a TABOO theme, but for me it is something normal and as such I incorporate it into my drawings and comics without any hang-ups.

LS: Even to the point of being equally comfortable drawing heterosexual erotica as well. As a gay man, is it difficult to imagine these heterosexual scenes?

IA: Turning on a heterosexual is very easy... They're very simple. I'm not talking about women, but rather men, who are the major consumers of erotic comics. Show them a pair of tits and a piece of ass and they're already hard. I'm a bit cruel, I know, but it's the truth. Nonetheless, whenever I've drawn heterosexual comics I've tried to create situations that could turn

ISMAEL ÁLVAREZ

myself on as well, just changing two gays for a heterosexual couple. I've also drawn lesbian duos, although since they were for a heterosexual male audience. They were those porcelain blondes with impossible curves... the kind that appeals to the Iberian macho.

LS: What does your family think about your explicit work?

IA: They support me 100%. My mother has always been very proud of me. It's not like she's going to hang one of my sex scenes on the fridge, but that's not necessary either. And she has always boasted of my artistic talent.

LS: Your art generally features young and muscular boys. What type of guy attracts you in real life?

IA: I won't deny that if my inky hunks became flesh and blood I'd be the happiest man in the world, but the truth is I'm not usually so extremist and don't have a single prototype of man I find attractive. I like tall guys, short ones, muscled guys, thin guys... Although I must say that my boyfriend is tall, like I am, handsome and defined... I guess I do like guys like in my drawings!

LS: You must have seen many naked men in order to draw the male body with such precision....

IA: I've seen plenty, I can't deny. To work well one must do one's research. Nonetheless, it helps a lot to have a continuous supply of reference material, and I generally imagine scenes with the help of photographs that I've taken myself or with material from other photographers.

LS: Who are some of your artistic inspirations?

IA: Without a doubt Tom of Finland is one of the great masters. I remember the first time I saw one of his drawings, at the tender age of eleven. A shiver ran along my body, from the tips of my toes up to my ears, passing through an incredible erection that the sight of such well-drawn potent men evoked in me. Since then I've sought out more material by him and he has been an inspiration to me from the beginning.

But I'm also like a sponge, absorbing from here and there all sorts of styles, which later become transformed into something of my own. As a result there are an infinite number of less-evident influences, such as the wonderful painter Gustav Klimt, the novels of Anne Rice, manga, etc.

LS: What can we look forward to from your pen (and monitor)?

IA: In terms of gay comics, I've finished a second episode for Patrick Fillion's RAPTURE titled "Be Careful What You Wish For." And I've an ongoing series titled "Only for Boys" in the Spanish magazine Claro Que Sí. I've also recently illustrated a (heterosexual) erotic tarot deck. Also in the works is an erotic lesbian graphic novel about dildos and vibrators written by Linda Álvarez (no relation) titled THE JOY OF TOYS. So a little of everything!

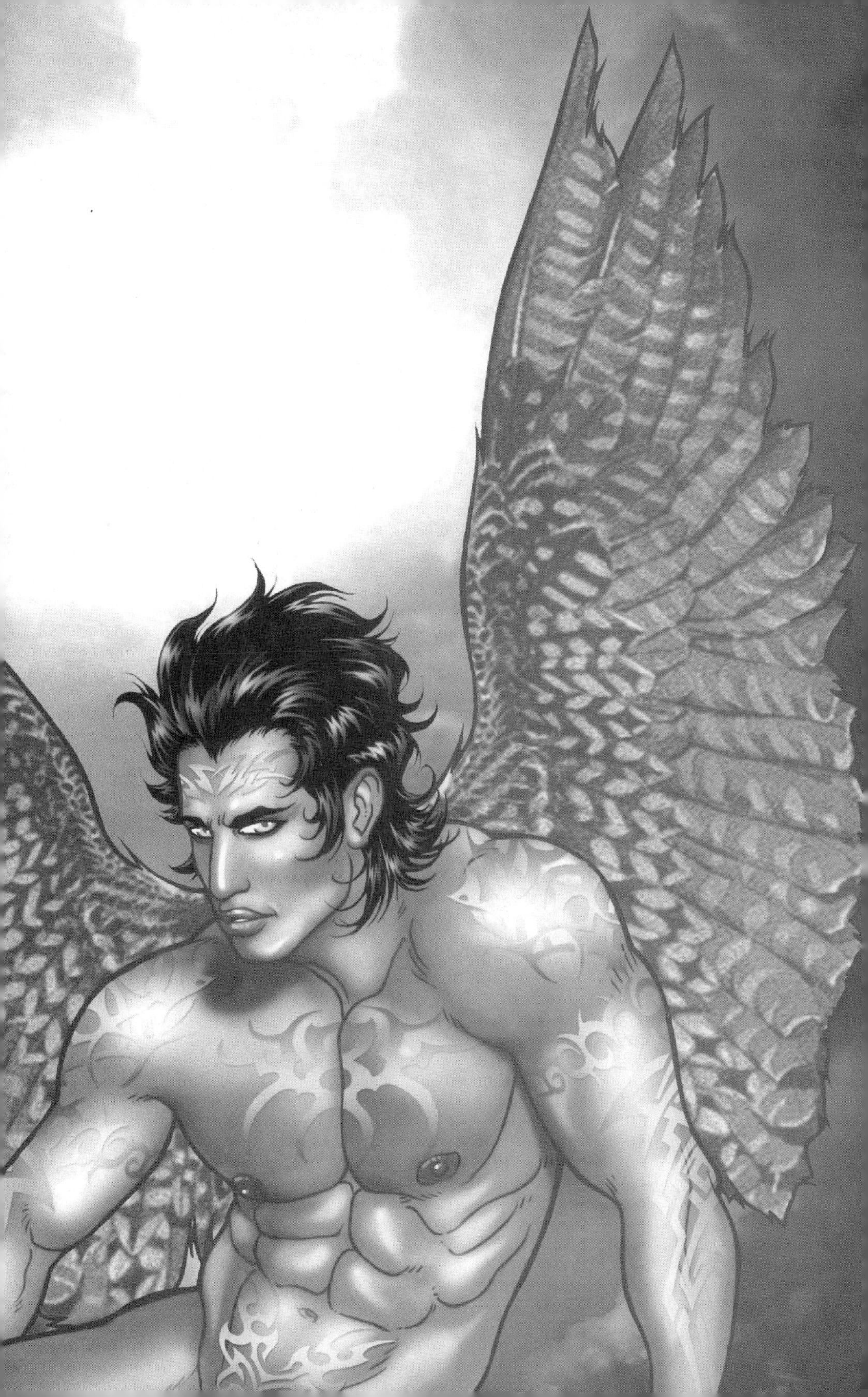

Cute Girls and Talking Monkeys: The Colleen Coover Interview by Justin Hall

Colleen Coover draws some of the cutest girls in comic books. To make matters even better, they love sex and love to get it on with each other! **SMALL FAVORS**, published by Eros Comix, is a rarity in erotic comic books, being sex-positive, completely queer, and featuring the work of a remarkably talented cartoonist at the top of her game.

Recently, Coover has collaborated with her partner, who goes by the nom de plume **Root Nibot**, on **BANANA SUNDAY**, published by Oni Press. The book features three mysterious talking monkeys and their human caretaker enrolling in a local high school. It showcases more of Coover's engaging artwork, as she expands her visual repertoire to boys and monkeys alongside her trademark cute girls.

a book that could
be enjoyed by women
who identify as lesbians
on an equal footing,
fantasy-wise, as bi or
straight women
and men

Justin Hall: Colleen, you're bisexual, and in fact you're involved with a man now, but SMALL FAVORS only features women. Why does the series only speak to one side of your sexuality?

Colleen Coover: The short answer is I just plain enjoy all-woman porn more. The long answer is that I wanted to make sure that this was a book that could be enjoyed by women who identify as lesbians on an equal footing, fantasy-wise, as bi or straight women and men. By not including any sex with men—by leaving out male characters altogether—the question of a character's sexual identity is left up to the reader to answer.

JH: What's it like working with a writer on BANANA SUNDAY? Have you ever worked with a collaborator before?

CC: I have worked with a writer before. In fact, Root Nibot, who usually works under his given name Paul Tobin, is the only other writer I've worked with in comics. In fact, he's my boyfriend. Before I did SMALL FAVORS, the only comics work I had done were short pieces for his anthology book ATTITUDE LAD, which was published by Slave Labor for three issues in the late '90s. He worked closely with me on much of the writing for SMALL FAVORS, so working on BANANA SUNDAY from a script that he's written feels entirely natural to me. I think we compliment each other nicely.

JH: BANANA SUNDAY is all-ages. Do you approach illustrating it differently than SMALL FAVORS? Do you only work on one book at a time to keep a mood going, or switch off between pages?

CC: No, there's no real difference, other than content. Once I lay out a page and figure out how to tell the story at hand, most of the actual drawing is about making things look right, getting lines down on the page. I only work on one book at a time because I have difficulty focusing on more than one project at a time. I can sometimes work on a painting and a comic at the same time, but I think that's only because you have to put a painting aside from time to time to let it dry.

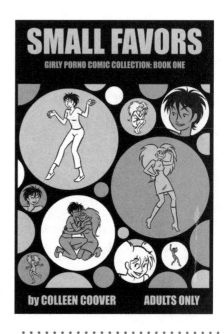

Enjoy an excerpt from Coover's SMALL FAVORS

YURIKO IS HAVING A COSTUME PARTY! **FANTASTIC!** I CAN... HEY, LOOK AT THIS...

Yuriko Manabe and Janus invite you to a Costume Party!

Naughty costumes are allowed. Refreshments will be served.

PLEASE BRING NIBBIL + SAGE!

HOW'D YURIKO KNOW THAT **SAGE** WOULD BE HERE?

EASY! JANUS IS A PART OF YOUR CONSCIENCE, SO SHE KNOWS A LOT OF STUFF **YOU** KNOW. WE'VE BEEN SLEEPING WITH SAGE.

NOT BEEN DOING MUCH SLEEPIN'...

...OKAY, I GET IT. JANUS TOLD YURIKO ABOUT... **HEY!** WHAT'S **JANUS** DOING WITH **YURIKO?** WHY ARE THE TWO OF THEM... **TOGETHER**... OH, MY GOD...

Oh my god.

MY **CONSCIENCE** IS SLEEPING WITH YURIKO AND **I'M NOT!!!**

LOOKS THAT WAY!

OH BOY! A COSTUME PARTY! I CAN BE A NINJA OR A QUEEN OR A BIG TOADSTOOL OR A SAILOR OR A HORSE OR A PLATE OF COLESLAW OR..

I CAN BE A KNIGHT OR A COWBOY OR AN ASTRONAUT OR A RACE CAR DRIVER OR A GIANT CRAB...

SO UNFAIR..

WE NEED TO GO **SHOPPING!**

JH: You're also a fine artist, and have had gallery shows of your paintings. How would you describe that work? Is it influenced by your comics art?

CC: I approach painting in pretty much the same way as comics; my goal is always to tell a story. I think I'm more of an illustrator than anything—the subjects of my last series of paintings were all characters from myth or folklore. I like staying within my own cartoony style, just with more depth and col-

or. I mostly work in watercolor and gouache, but I'd like to start experimenting with other media, like acrylic or cel vinyl.

JH: Two years ago you were on the first Queer Cartoonists panel at the Alternative Press Expo, which I moderated. I received an email from an audience member upset that a pornographer was on the panel, and that your inclusion perpetrated negative stereotypes of queer communities as obsessed with sex. How do you respond to that?

CC: Wow, I had no idea! I don't remember what all was said during that panel, but I know we talked about SMALL FAVORS and comics in general without going into any explicit detail. I think it's unfortunate that such a stereotype about queer people exists, but I don't think that should make us afraid to discuss sex and sexual entertainment like grown-ups.

JH: You draw some of the cutest girls around. Who do you think draws the cutest boys in comics?

CC: My tastes in male beauty tend to be kind of old-fashioned. I prefer rugged handsomeness to prettiness, lean muscle to bulk, and a well-draped suit to skin-tight spandex. My favorite cartoonist of all time is Milton Caniff, but when it comes to artists working today, Jaime Hernandez and Darwyn Cooke are the tops in drawing hunky fellas.

Enjoy an excerpt from
SMALL FAVORS

JH: Where can we find your comics and art, and do you have any other projects in the works?

CC: I have a story in the all-woman anthology SEXY CHIX edited by Diana Schutz, that came out in December from Dark Horse. I've got one painting that'll be published in Craig Yoe's upcoming book ARF MUSEUM. and another in a book of work by a large number of really hot artists being put together by Jacob Covey for Fantagraphics—I'm not sure what the title will be for that one. I've been doing some illustrations for magazines, notably Nickelodeon Magazine, which is always fun. I did an illustration for a short prose story by Paul Tobin that will be published in the literary journal Spork. I always have art for sale on ComicArtCollective.com, and I often post images on my Live Journal (username: colleencoover). Finally, I'm currently working on a couple of comics pieces; one short story and one that's more like a novella, both written by Paul Tobin.

THE 3rd ACT with DEVIN GRAYSON

BY LYLE MASAKI

When Devin Grayson's work first appeared in one-shot specials and annuals for DC, online fans quickly took notice of her distinct character-focused writing style. Her writing quickly earned her a following and a long term assignment on CATWOMAN, her first Bat-title with many to follow. You may have seen Grayson's work in titles like NIGHTWING, BATMAN: GOTHAM KNIGHTS, BLACK WIDOW and THE TITANS. Grayson has also worked on creator-owned projects like RELATIVE HEROES, USER and, most recently, MATADOR.

Hearing Devin Grayson talk about the comic industry and comics always turns into a stimulating experience, as she usually has some sharp insights to deliver. I was pretty excited to have the chance to discuss some of her experiences with introducing LGBT characters, gaming communities and the challenges of working with franchise properties.

. . . .

LYLE MASAKI: In a recent interview you talked about the limitations of writing in the comics industry, where major characters have to remain relatively unchanged so that the licensing possibilities remain wide open. How do you approach characters who cannot see a lot of long-term development and tell interesting stories about them?

DEVIN GRAYSON: Well, one thing these characters do have in abundance is past; fantastic, complicated, intricate, compelling, story-rich pasts. Entire dramas can be created out of re-examinations of old relationships, betrayals, re-alliances, reunions, and romances. As long as the material mined from there remains accessible to newer readers (which is a relatively simple manner of thoughtful exposition), it can sometimes provide even more story potential than an open future. To over-simply, the future is what happens to a character, just a series of incidents that test their nature, but their past is what gives them that character and defines the box of tools they're going to have available when confronted with a new situation.

In the superhero genre, as well, there is always the over-arcing theme of good versus evil. Even if you know that the hero is almost always going to weigh in on the side of good, there are a lot of intense stories that can be told about the nature of those forces, and the ways in which we embrace, challenge, face, and ultimately integrate them. When Batman gets into a fight, for example, you can feel pretty confident that he's going to win by story's end, but you don't know how or at what cost.

In a way, too, by virtue of being legends, these characters are frozen in time. That allows for a nearly endless game of "what if"; how would he respond to this, how would she get out of that? Then, of course, when you least expect it, we do move someone forward or completely decimate their status quo. And that's done on a regular basis, too, in what you might call the comic book Act II – that's the point in the story where everything goes so wrong, the reader can't imagine how it will ever get put back together. But it is put back together – every single time, by Act III, without fail (allowing for the fact that Act III can occur anywhere from page twenty-one of the same issue to a miniseries eight years later). As long as you know how to get back to Act III, the things you can do in Act II are fairly limitless. This ritualistic, serialized mode of story telling is actually one of my favorites. We have everything we need: history, conflicts, and even magic (am I wrong, or does the return of Jason Todd and Bucky set the odds-of-coming-back-if-killed-in-a-comic at a clean 100%?). There's always amazing amounts of potential in characters people have been developing and investing in for years, with the possibilities almost always outweighing the restrictions. That's why so many of us have stories of their own about these characters they're dying to tell.

LM: One thing that makes Dick Grayson such a compelling characters to me is that he's one of the few major characters in the DC Universe to have gone through so many life changes. We've seen him change over time. Considering how DC series will jump forward one year in time after INFINITE CRISIS ends, it seems the time is ripe for Nightwing to enter another phase in his life. Will we get to see a new day for the former Boy Wonder?

DG: I would imagine so. I think the idea is to really shake things up and see a lot of places and characters in ways we've never seen them before, which is what makes the idea so interesting.

LM: I remember seeing you talk at a Gays in Comics panel where you said that you felt obliged to include lesbian and gay characters in your writing because the writer's job is to reflect reality and LGBT people are a part of reality. However, when writing for a superhero universe there are additional hurdles towards putting a diverse cast together. The large number of established characters makes it challenging to introduce a gay character since the new character has to bring something, creatively, that an existing character cannot bring or else face charges of tokenism. What have been the challenges you've faced in reflecting the diversity found in real life?

DG: Well, you have a point, but I'd argue that this isn't so much a problem with sexuality—since any established or new character could quite suddenly and legitimately decide to explore and/or confess a previously uncharted part of his or her true nature—as with something like racial diversity. It's not tokenism if the revelation and/or transition makes sense for the character and the story, but it would be difficult, for example, to change the racial configuration of a comic book universe overnight for the simple fact that once established as white, it's damn tricky to arrange for a character wake up Asian, Latin, black or what have you, whereas I think a perfectly good case could be made for one or two of our better known characters to one day wake up gay.

NIGHTWING

Still, I know that the efforts to introduce new and lasting characters of a more diverse nature—sexually, racially, and culturally—on the part of all the people I work with have been effective and sincere. More needs to be done, of course, but I feel confident that these efforts will continue. So confident, in fact, that I dearly hope you're still following my work next summer.... J

LM: I loved your Vertigo mini-series USER when it came out for being a great character-driven story with stunning art. USER focused on a young woman who discovered an online gaming community, a discovery that helps her escape from her troubles. In the community she plays the role of a male knight in a relationship with another man -- who it turns out, is also being roleplayed by a woman. It was a very mature depiction of a character's sexual awakening, one that was rare in comics at the time USER was published. USER also seemed rare as a comic that focused on its lead character's personal growth without any big action scenes. Do you think that rarity is because of the visual nature or comics or because the industry is going through a cycle where there's less interest in that sort of character-focused comic?

DG: Interesting question. First of all, thank you for the kind words about USER, that project means a lot to me. In an attempt to answer, I'm just guessing, but from my perspective, I'd say both things are true. We were so lucky with USER to have both John Bolton and Sean Phillips bringing that world to life – there are scenes in suburban kitchens and virtual bars in that story more resplendent and visually compelling than the most ornate fight scenes I've ever written–you can certainly imagine how much that story could have lost in the hands of less talented artists. USER is not a superhero story, and there has been a kind of renaissance recently of the very continuity-heavy, aimed-straight-at-the-heart-of-the-fan-boy kind of story telling, but there's always room in publishing for complete tangents as long as the story itself is strong enough. MATADOR, which Brian Stelfreeze and I have been doing over at Wildstorm, isn't a typical superhero story in the least, and Wildstorm was very enthusiastic about it from the beginning and continue to be hugely supportive to this day. So I think it's probably accurate to point toward an overall trend toward bigger action and more traditional mainstream material, but I also think there are always ways to get other kind of stories made if you believe in what you're doing.

Or at least if you can get Brian Stelfreeze to believe in what you're doing. ;-)

LM: Looking back at USER has me wondering–online gaming communities have changed since that mini-series was published and there are now plenty of online games slickly made from major software developers. Do you still participate in gaming communities and has your participation changed since then?

DG: I admit it; I've been sucked in by the eye candy. I still play online roll playing games avidly (and even still have Dallian—Guilliame's "real life" counter part—rolled up as a PC) but now I participate in avatar-driven MMORPGs and continue to play character-sheet and dice living room RPs once a week with a group of old friends. One of my PCs is even female. I haven't participated in a text-based MOO like the one depicted in USER for years, though I'm still in touch with some of the people from that game (Dallian's guild commander—Arhia in USER—created and currently manages my website, for example).

LM: I remember when RELATIVE HEROES came out there were rumors that you faced editorial interference over the outing of the team's leader, Huston. Do you think times have changed since then, have some of the hurdles towards outing a major character been removed?

DG: Well, in this case, those rumors are untrue. I don't remember anyone having a problem with Huston being gay – there was even a twelve-month outline (the story was eventually approved as a six-part miniseries) that continued developing the relationship between Joel (Huston) and Rive and no one ever asked me to change it. The only thing we argued over was the title–we had been calling the story "The Weinbergs" in-house, but eventually a decision was made to release it as "Relative Heroes," and my only objection to that was that I felt it made the mini sound a lot more mainstream than it was ever intended to be. But even that was a marketing decision. It had nothing to do with political oppression of any kind.

RELATIVE HEROES

In terms of whether or not times have changed, I think there's been a slow, continual progression, and that actually things are moving at a reasonable and acceptable speed. It's not just an editor or a publishing house–recognition of gay identity is a national issue that I think overall you'd have to say fiction is currently handling with more alacrity and honesty than real-world politics. In the case of DC in particular, suffice to say that just last month I had a meeting with the powers that be to discuss introducing a little more sexual diversity into the capes and tights set, and by the end of the meeting, we had agreed on a course of action that every single one of us was pleased with. It may seem quiet out there right now from your perspective, but progression is happening, and the wheels are turning even as we speak.

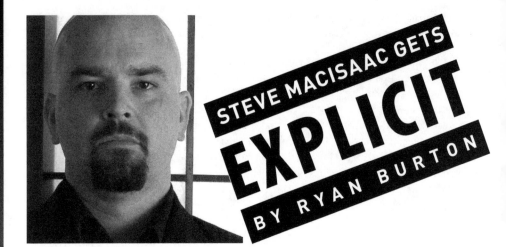

STEVE MACISAAC GETS EXPLICIT
BY RYAN BURTON

He's been STICKY for his fans and he'll be a SHIRTLIFTER for his critics, but he'll never forget to bring the needed touch of erotica. Canadian-born, California-living Steve MacIsaac talks about his inspirations, the men in his stories, and how he'll now longer try to second-guess his audience.

. . . .

Ryan Burton: Being a gay erotic comic illustrator anywhere seems like a pretty tough gig. But Japan? Was there a market for gay erotica in the Land of the Rising Sun?

Steve MacIsaac: Actually, the reason I started was because I thought it would be easier than in North America, since unlike North America, the gay monthly magazines routinely feature between 40-80 pages of comics as part of the mix. One of the original reasons we decided to keep STICKY wordless was in the hopes of getting picked up there, and we wanted to avoid translation issues. Not that it worked--the first version of "Talk Show Queers", the only thing I submitted, was rejected. Not that surprisingly, really—my storytelling approach is not particularly Japanese, and content wise, we were simultaneously too explicit and too tame compared to what was in most of the comics in gay magazines.

RB: So then I guess it's safe to assume you're having more luck in the Land of the Brave, Home of the Free...? I mean, those who live in the States and are familiar with your work on STICKY are certainly looking forward to SHIRTLIFTER...

SM: Yes, and I am grateful to all 10 of you. I guess it depends on what you mean by luck. I'm happy to be published and everything, and certainly I am grateful to have work published and out there. Mostly I do comics because I like drawing them, and it's a bonus when people like what I do. I'm grateful to everyone who's bought one of my comics. But it's not like STICKY was a great financial success or anything. It got a lot of positive press, but most of it [was] in the non-comics media, and ultimately not very many people actually saw it. Hopefully that will change with the upcoming collection, which will actually be available in gay bookstores–something we weren't able to do with the single issues.

RB: How big will the STICKY collection be? And what can your audience expect from SHIRTLIFTER?

SM: The STICKY collection will be 80 pages-- all three issues and covers, plus 4 or 5 pages of new material. SHIRTLIFTER will be a very different thing. There will be sex present at times, and although at times it might be explicit, especially in some of the reprinted material, it's not porn, really–the primary function isn't to try and get you off. The focus is much more on narrative, telling stories, and will be more character driven than my previous work, both in STICKY or in the solo pieces I have done for various anthologies.

RB: I see, but how will you go about focusing on the characterization of your subjects and not the sex? And does the notion of having character driven stories stem from your personnel tastes or that of your audience?

SM: Well, I've never been exclusively an erotic cartoonist. Although sex is certainly present in the solo pieces I've done, those strips were usually to a great extent about the main character's relationship to sex, the role it plays in his life, and usually to some extent the roles depicted have been somewhat ambivalent. STICKY's a contrast to that--gay manic depressives having sex isn't a particularly winning formula for a f— book, so Dale and I try to keep the tone fairly positive and light. But both there and with SHIRTLIFTER I'm doing things that interest me, not trying to second guess my "audience", since I have no idea who my audience is. If people are interested in SHIRTLIFTER, great, but I'm not doing it to please other people. That said, hopefully there's enough people who like what I do that I can keep it going. As to how I'll make the shift to more character-driven work, I guess by having things more dialogue-driven, letting stories emerge from character interaction and situations rather than by using narration, which has been a characteristic of my work in the past. Following people around for a while so you get to know them, rather than having them be ciphers who exist to make a particular narrative or political point.

RB: I couldn't help but notice--from what I've seen, most of your subjects are burly, muscular, beard-donning men's men. Is it a conscious decision on your part to draw your characters this way instead of, say, the often-portrayed, stereotypical effeminate male?

SM: Well, that's been the case in STICKY, sure, though I think my palette's a little broader when it comes to my solo work. SHIRTLIFTER's going to be cut from a broader cloth, for example, and will feature a range of types, ages and ethnicities. But I would be lying if I said that I don't like drawing "burly, muscular, beard-donning men's men". I don't do it as a conscious, political decision, however–I'm not trying to make a point, I do it because with STICKY, it was a common ground that both Dale and I liked, and which IS representative of a very large part of gay culture.

RB: In September you became Prism Comics' recipient of its first annual Queer Press Grant. Did this come as somewhat of a shock to you? What happened when you were first told about it?

SM: I was pleasantly surprised and very honored when they told me that I had received the grant. The first thing that I did was tell my husband, who is a big comics fan and a supporter of my work.

RB: Did you use the money that you received from the grant to jumpstart SHIRTLIFTER, or did you and your husband use it to celebrate? Be honest.

SM: I put a bit of the grant towards a good color printer for proofing, but the majority is still sitting there, waiting to be put towards the cost of putting out the first issue. I was pretty sick when we got the news, so there wasn't much celebrating to be had. Well, I guess I did buy a slightly more expensive box of Kleenex, now that I think about it...

RB: No celebrating for the wicked, I guess. As an artist and a writer where do you find your inspiration when dealing with the issues and scenarios you address in your work?

SM: Well, with STICKY it's easy--I follow the script that Dale sends me. I mean, he goes over some of the possible scenarios beforehand to see if I'm interested, but basically my job on STICKY was to interpret his script,

building and adding upon it when necessary, but always within the parameters of what he's outlined. With my own work, my inspiration more or less comes from life, although not necessarily mine: aside from the piece I contributed to TRUE PORN, I don't do autobiography. Even then, it was filtered through a lens of fantasy, in the sense that my idea was to juxtapose events from my real life and "the road not taken"--sort of like a gay "What If..." story. But mostly as a writer I take events and situations I've heard about and use them as a departure point for my own spin on it. The story "Crush" that's coming out in BEST OF BOY TROUBLE next year is like that–based on something that happened to a friend of mine. The premise of the story is based on a real event, but everything else is made up. And that's definitely the case with the first story in SHIFTLIFTER. It's vaguely based on the situation of someone I knew briefly, but aside from the basic idea it's completely fictional.

RB: When you do use your friends' stories--do you let them know in advance, or do they have to pick up your work to find out?

SM: Well, with "Crush" I did, because it was someone that is, in fact a friend, and was someone I was living with. Other times it would depend on how close it skews to reality, which generally isn't very much. The main

story in SHIRTLIFTER, for example, isn't based on someone I know very well, or even in contact with anymore–I wouldn't know how to get ahold of him. And "based on" is a probably too strong, in any event–the only thing that is common is that the guy had a boyfriend who was a corporate executive, and had a tendency to be unfaithful. Everything else in the story—the details of their relationship, their family background, their ethnicities—is complete fiction, and is not at all an attempt to tell their story. It's more accurate to say that their situation started me thinking about question of faithfulness, isolation, and obligation, thinking about to what extent are we responsible for and to other people. The story I'm telling is based on my explorations around that question, not an attempt to describe their lives.

RB: In WHAT'S WRONG? you contributed an erotic strip that dealt with anti-censorship, and on one of the pages you write, "Consumption of pornography harms oneself as well as others". Can you elaborate?

SM: That strip sometimes confuses people, and I think you have to look at it in the context. WHAT'S WRONG? was an anti-censorship book, and was surrounded by lots and lots of other free speech and anti-censorship comics, so I think that affects your reading of the strip. Outside that context, it is prone to being misunderstood as somehow pro-censorship, which was not my intent. When you read the slogan you mention above—or any of the other slogans I used, which were more or less distillations of a variety of pro-censorship positions, porn harms minors, porn causes sexual deviation, etc, etc.—and then you look at the images each slogan is juxtaposed against, which are all more or less celebratory depictions of people engaging in sexual activity. The purpose was to create a kind of tension, a dissonance between the words and the images that accompany them, to undercut the slogans with positive depictions of sexual activity. But given the limitations of my drawing at the time, a lot of people misunderstand it, and read it as a straight anti-porn indictment, which sort of indicates that it wasn't entirely successful at doing that.

RB: But do you feel you've found your niche in erotica, or do you want to spread you wings a little and try your hand at other genres?

SM: Well, the answer to both questions is yes. I think I have found a niche in erotica--I'm not planning to abandon doing erotic work. But all along I have worked on stories that were not intended specifically as erotica. For the past three years mostly that kind of work has taken a back seat while I worked on STICKY. Now I'd like to focus on it a little bit more, play with some other approaches before I do another erotic story again. Which is not to say there won't be [a] sexual element to the work I'm doing–it's there. But it's not going to be porn.

RB: Are we talking mature superheroes and not bumbling idiots in spandex? Gay cowboys? Promiscuous teens fighting some Dr. Doom knockoff? Or just everyday life?

SM: I really don't have a lot of interest in doing superheroes. I'll read a certain amount of that kind of stuff if it's done well--I liked Morrison and Quitely's X-MEN–but I really don't think I have much to add to that genre that hasn't

already been done before. The first serial in SHIRTLIFTER is, I guess you would call it slice of life. It's basically concerned with a guy who came to Japan to be with his boyfriend, who got a great job there. He's bored out of his skull, underemployed, and as a result prone to serial infidelity. A lot of the story deals with his attempts to deal with his growing sense of alienation–from his job, from the country he's living in, and increasingly from his boyfriend. So it's everyday life, in the sense of someone dealing with personal issues. But in doing that I'm not interested in trying to "represent" the gay community in some way, in the sense of trying to reflect a certain lifestyle or set of living circumstances. I'm not trying to direct it at a specific demographic group to try and confirm their idea of "normal". I'm just trying to tell stories that interest me.

RB: It's funny you should mention Morrison--he caught some flack when he donned the X-Men in leather. I happen to think that they've never looked greater or sexier. But on the subject of what interests you, what would you tell aspiring writers or artists: write/draw for yourself, or write/draw for your audience?

SM: I think second-guessing what people want of you is a mug's game. People can spot insincerity from a thousand miles away. That doesn't mean that I think there's no such thing as self-indulgence, or that sincerity is enough: lots of horrible comics have been done with absolute earnestness. But good work invariably exists because it is something the cartoonist wills into existence. You can immediately tell the difference between something that the creators are engaged in, and a cynical marketing exercise.

RB: I know this is totally cliché, Steve, but what type of advice do you have for people starting out in print media?

SM: Ummmm....Don't do it? Seriously, I'm not sure I'm the best person to ask--certainly not if one of the intents of the question is "How do you make a living at it?" Because I certainly don't. •

"We are the myth-writers of the day"

—Terry Moore's Personal Paradise
by Sean McGrath

Ah! Terry Moore's STRANGERS IN PARADISE – more complex than parabolic geometry, yet able to touch the hearts of a wide and diverse readership as easily as a puppy. When Prism Comics offered me the chance to interview Terry, I jumped at it, hoping to get a better feel for the creator of this outrageously human and loving story.

Sean McGrath: Reading STRANGERS IN PARADISE, I'd have to say that the idea of love permeates the story. Do you think that love transcends gender or even sexual identity? SIP is at the same time perfectly simple and alarmingly complicated. The way Katchoo and Francine and David reveal themselves to one another (and to us) continually reinforces the idea of their love for each other. They're not coy, nor are they naive. In SIP, do we glimpse some of Terry Moore's personal philosophy about human relationships?

Terry Moore: All the good stuff reflects on me, all the bad stuff must be somebody else. Seriously, I have my thoughts of course, but I am subordinate to the characters. They are not like me in many ways, so it is important for me to not get in the way. If fiction was just a way to put yourself out there using puppets on paper I wouldn't want to be a part of it. Creating fiction or paintings or what have you, it is a strange process that non-creating people don't understand, hence all the questions about it. But the artist is the source of something greater than himself, making things that come from him but that are better than him and usually quite different. So SIP is not me. I love it and I love the characters, but they don't love me back.

SM: Alice Walker says something along the same lines - that she is a vessel of story-telling, the characters are the ones who tell the story through her. So, maybe you can indeed blame the bad

stuff on your characters and say, "Hey, their lives, not mine!" At a school I used to work at, all the guy teachers would gather at lunch time to watch Days of Our Lives. The odd thing was they were all the sports coaches! Has SIP enjoyed a similar following?

TM: Half my readers are women, so the other half has some explaining to do, I guess. SIP readers are all types of people on the outside. Inside I think they care for people and value relationships.

SM: On a related note, what do you think is the biggest draw of STRANGERS IN PARADISE to men - gay and straight? Women - gay and straight?

TM: I hope the appeal is a good story. Something worth reading, worth looking at and pondering after the read.

SM: What do you think is the future of GLBT characters in comics?

TM: I think they will be absorbed into society and literature to the point of complete acceptance. Literature can help with that, allowing people to come to know and care for others not like them-selves. Think of the families that love and accept a GLBT member. A society can do likewise when people feel the connection to others and get to know them through the arts and literature.

SM: I picked up SIP #1 back when I was in college at the recommendation of a friend. She said it was "bold and daring" and that it "pioneered GLBT comics". And in the early 90's there was so little for GLBT folk to read and relate to and feel... well, acceptable. I remember when I read SiP that it wasn't just "gay/straight", in fact, I remember my 22 year old mind being confused by how it wasn't just "gay/straight", but this swirl of feelings between these three people. Do you feel like a pioneer for the GLBT community as far as promoting acceptance through literature or was/is SIP just good storytelling to you?

TM: The only strong feeling I had about "the great divide" at the time was that I thought dividing the world into two camps was stupid and short-sighted. Nothing is black and white, not people, sex, politics, faith. The attempt to do so just adds to and prolongs the confusion — it's not the answer. I know love and sex is more than man-woman, love-hate, attraction-contempt. So I write from my heart on these matters and ignore whatever is the social viewpoint of the summer.

SM: I've read that you have ideas about bringing the real and the fantastical together in comics (i.e., "The Physics of Superman"). How soon could we expect to see something along those lines from you, whether through DC or Indy work?

TM: Maybe after SIP.

SM: Oh no! Does this mean SiP may end soon?

TM: Yes, it will end May 2007 with issue 90. If I don't bring the story to a strong ending it will never be considered a good story, but instead be seen in retrospective as a rambling tale that lacks definition. I would hate to spend 14 years of my life on SIP and end up with such a vague legacy, so it's time.

SM: Do you think SIP could ever make it as a movie–not only in terms of popularity, but also in terms of translation? Would you trust the Hollywood Machine with SIP?

TM: No, I wouldn't trust Hollywood. I would trust New York's film makers though. The strong indie film makers would know what to do with this. I know SIP would make a strong film because we have so much story to draw from.

Terry and I met for the in-person part of the interview at the Wizard World Con in Arlington, TX where he was doing work for ACTOR ("A Commitment to Our Roots") and I was busy spending lots and lots of money and promoting a studio I work for. We sat in a hallway in the "Staff Only" area, trying to have a few quiet minutes of Q&A. One thing that anyone who talks with Terry has to notice first is his sense of humor; the second thing would have to be his sincere earnestness about everything his says. Both of these make him an easy person to talk with.

SM: How did you get involved in with ACTOR and when did it start up?

TM: After it was brought to my attention by my friend Jim McLauchlin, who is the senior editor at Top Cow and I knew him back when he was with Wizard, that there was a charity now to help old comic book creators who did not now have retirement funds and needed assistance with the logistics of life. And I thought that's very nice. ACTOR is the charity that takes that responsibility on itself. Since I will probably need ACTOR someday, I will support that. So when I go to conventions a lot of times I'll do some sketches [to get donations for ACTOR]. In this particular show ACTOR brought me in just to sketch for them. It's the last show of the season for me, and, you know, I've done all these shows this year for STRANGERS IN PARADISE, so I thought I'd do one show for somebody else.

SM: That's very nice of you. It's something I've never considered–people in comics, what do they do once they retire, if they retire at all? I mean, I can't think of a single person that's "retired" from comics. They just kind of pick another career or they work right up until the day they die, and then that's it.

TM: It's because there's not much attention paid to it. A person reaches a point in his career when people stop paying attention. A lot of these guys just fade away. They have no more income, no more jobs, and I don't know what they live on. Everyone has their own story. So those are the guys that need help. You know there's no retirement fund, or insurance plan or 401Ks in comics, nothing like that. So, they're on their own, unless they're fortunate enough to have hit something and make some income. When you're done, you're done, and you have nothing left to show for it but your work. It's nice but it doesn't buy you medicine when you're 80.

SM: Or hospital care or nursing care or a hospice bed.

TM: Exactly.

SM: Given [a career in comics] or a "normal life" which would be preferable to you? Having the security of... well, we say "security" but as a high school teacher I don't see a lot of security in my 401K (not that I have a 401K) but in whatever it is the state does for me, and Social Security.

TM: I don't think I have any choice because I've had three careers so far. This is my third career, and my middle career was the closest I've ever come to "normal life," which was a TV editor. And

I didn't fit. I was a negative magnet in a barrel of positive magnets, and they just popped me out. The whole time I was in there it was all chaos and friction … before that I was a rock musician and now I'm a cartoonist. It fits well with me and I'm with my kind. Life seems normal to me.

SM: I was reading an article from a few years ago that said you wanted to make an SIP music CD. Is that still a viable project?

TM: Oh, yeah, it's a pet project of mine. There's a lot of logistics involved in making that happen, so I've been working on that on the side. It's still something I'd like to do. The interview DVD that's out has some of the music on there. One piece that's on there (and on my website as well) that's outstanding is "This Mask I Wear." Desha Dunnahoe wrote music to it, and it's just gorgeous.

SM: Would you want to have one person make the recordings of your songs like Berke Breathed did for *Billy and the Boingers* or more like a tribute CD with multiple artists along the lines of *I Wanna Be a Carpenter?*

TM: I would do several artists, totally different styles—everything from punk to bluegrass—and have them do Griffin's solo music. So, it would be a diverse album.

SM: Excellent, excellent. What about this coming year? Besides SIP, I know you said you were going to wrap it up by issue 90, so, what else is out there for you in 2006?

TM: 2006 I'll be totally focused on SIP, and I'm going to put all my focus on ending it with a huge bang, making a great finish to a series I spent twelve years on. It's very important to me I give it a strong ending, so it is seen in retrospect as a strong story. If it has a great ending that will bear well on the entire thing, and that's really important to me now. I gave it a strong beginning, a complex middle and now it needs a strong ending. When it does that, I think I will have something that will be able to stand on its own.

SM: I daresay. Everything you've written so far is, as you said, very complex. There are times in the series when we actually jump into the future, we see ten years into the future with Francine and Katchoo and their being separated for so long, Francine with a daughter and living with her Mom. Is that going to figure in as well? I mean, having see past the end, the end has to be even bigger than that.

TM: I am redefining the end. When 9/11 happened, I rethought my role as a writer writing entertainment fiction. The aftermath of 9/11 made me feel a burden of responsibility to capture the essence of humanity in my stories, capture the essence of our souls. Not in Humanity the Big Picture, but in the little things like each individual's heart and soul. I've tried to do that in my stories but I also feel a mantle of responsibility to instill hope. I think hope comes from the poets and writers and the heroes and what they create. We're able to puncture all of our real-life heroes, it's just what people do, but it's hard to pick apart our literary heroes. They become more iconographic throughout time and I think each writer has a real responsibility. The comic book writers of the day are the ones perpetuating the contemporary heroes. We are the myth-writers of the day; we are the Grimms and Greek storytellers; we are Edgar Allen Poe; we are F. Scott Fitzgerald and Hemmingway because there's nowhere else for those guys to work now. The "real" book industry is all about how-to books or big hits. There is no place for short story writers… I guess they really don't print short stories the way they used to, which is where all [the great writ-

A DISTANT SCREAM

SOMEDAYS I THINK
I'M GOING TO GIVE IT ALL AWAY
FIND A JOB THAT PAYS
SOME LETTERS BEHIND MY NAME.

SOMEDAYS I'LL BE
STANDING AT A MIRROR LOOKING IN
YOUR FACE STARTS FADING IN
THE FEELING COMES AGAIN.

I GUESS I'LL ALWAYS BE
THE LOSING SIDE OF YOU.
YOUR MISMATCHED OTHER SHOE
YOUR AFTER MIDNIGHT BLUES.

LOVE IS A MYSTERY TO ME.
A LOSER'S DREAM.

THESE DAYS ARE SPENT
IN HOT DESIRE TO BE THE WAY I WAS.
TO RIDE THE MAGIC BUS
TO TRY AND STAY IN TOUCH.

AFRAID MY FACE
IS JUST A MEMORY TO THOSE I KNEW.
AN INFLUENTIAL CLUE
TO WHAT THEY HAVE TO LOSE.

I GUESS I'LL ALWAYS BE
THE LOSING SIDE OF YOU.
YOUR MISMATCHED OTHER SHOE
YOUR AFTER MIDNIGHT BLUES.

LOVE IS A MYSTERY.
TO ME, A DISTANT SCREAM.

ers] of the 20th century came from. There's nowhere for short story writers to go. Don't get me started. The book industry is not [catering] to them anymore, so a lot of the really good American fiction writers are working in comics. It's a good income and your story can be out immediately – untouched and unedited – to the reader base. [Comics] are a pipeline directly to the public. Once writers figure that out, a lot of them come to comics. That's why you see J. Michael Straczynski and Joss Whedon working in comics. You'd think, "Why are you working in this tiny pulp fiction niche?" Well, the reason is because they can write anything they want and it gets to the public within a month, and that is just an incredible lure for a writer. So, they come and they bring their original ideas, the ones that are maybe kind of a little out there, and they don't really want to have to go through a committee to approve them. They just want to write it as it is and put it out there.

SM: Two questions. For you, it's about coming away form the darkness. There was and still is a pretty big movement in comics to reveal the darker features of the heroes, to move them off their pedestals and make them, in some ways, worse than human. They're separate, independent, powerful and beyond liability. It's almost like we revel in their darkness. Classic example – Batman, and even what's happening right now with Superman and the Justice League. If you ever have seen Justice League on Cartoon Network, this past season was amazingly dark. There's a push for the darkness in our heroes. What you're saying is 9/11 was a turning point for you, where you went to the more hopeful side of life, where the stories that get told aren't all about the bad that people do, but about the good that can go on after them.

TM: Yeah. For me, what "darkness" means is "no hope," and if you pull that out of somebody, they die. What keeps us all going is hope in something. The reason Batman is such a dick right now is that everyone was so enchanted by the Dark Knight idea, but now it's been run into the ground. They've totally deconstructed anything that resembled the heroic Batman. It's that way with many characters, but I think you're going to see a shift in that. When I was at the Diamond retailers summit a month ago, DC was talking about their plans for 2006 with INFINITE CRISIS, which is going to wrap up every storyline and bring them to a big head. One the other side of that will be 2007, when all these characters who have had a serious reality check will, I think, undergo a "phoenix effect", rising from the ashes of disaster to become the heroes they are. And I think DC's goal is to put the heroism back into the characters. I'm very excited about that. One of the reasons I'm sick of darkness now is because I have a big anti-establishment streak in me, and now darkness is the establishment. That's where we are and I'm ready for the change. And that's what's happening in my book as well. I was heading for one type of ending, and I rethought it, [considering] not just my readership now but my readership 20 years from now, when someone says, "Read this book." I think about society and where our society is going, how my story fits in and if it's of any use to somebody 20, 30, 40 years from now. Why would you want to read it? It depends on what kind of a story is in there, about people and humanity and hope.

SM: Being an artist, does that make you political by default?

TM: I'm not interested in politics; I'm interested in sociology. I don't care about politics because I see that as transient. I'm interested in the flow of our society. I've studied every decade in American history. I have a feel for the continuity, the Golden Thread throughout it. I know what turns into our phases. It's the same things the stories do. I guess I'm interested in the history of people, where we night be going.

SM: Because I'm writing this for Prism, I have to ask, all the weird stuff that's going on in Texas and the nation – for example, the Klan is marching to Austin today [November 4, 2005] to show support for Proposition Two. With kind of flow, this event has been a long time in coming. When you first started writing SIP, I was in college, there was a movement towards a willingness to try to understand GLBT folks in society. Late-nineties the movement was more popular and gay characters started showing up on TV, in movies; and now there's this reaction to it in the other direction. Is that also part of the flow – the push and pull towards accepting differences among people?

TM: If you want to see the end of the Gay Rights Movement, look to Civil Rights. If you were to look to history for some lessons and guidelines, I would look to Civil Rights. I would hope that we're moving closer towards love and respect. It changed my life when I realized that if you treat everyone with care and respect everything goes wonderfully; your day goes well and your life walking through people goes well. Unfortunately, not everybody has that particular view. The very idea that in this day and age that there are still wars astounds me. War is such an old, barbaric way of handling something. When we went to war against Iraq, I just couldn't believe it. It's the most hateful, non-respectful way to solve an issue I've ever heard of in my life, and I can't believe Man is still doing that. Contrast that against two guys trying to find a marriage license somewhere in America; it makes their story look small, but they're both related [events]. They're trying to find acceptance and respect, same as everyone else in the world, in their own way. Until we start [respecting] each other, nothing is ever going to work out. We have all this friction. I think it's baby steps. It's astounding Man has been around as long as he has and it was only 85 years ago that we started allowing woman to come out of the delivery room or the kitchen. And it was only 40 years ago that we would allow a black person to sit next to a white person on a public bench. Unbelievably archaic progress! It's unacceptable. I think on the positive side that society as a whole is willing to accept anything they don't see as a threat. I think savvy, modern-day society wants to be accepting, you know, "live and let live", but they want to be sure it's not a threat. I think it's a long, slow process, but eventually we get there, and if we don't get there it'll be because the world blew up before we got there.

SM: Obviously you're about good literature and good stories. One last thing, indie comics, where are they now and where will they be going in the next year?

TM: I think we'll have some new publishers, the kind that four or five guys get together, make a couple of books themselves, form a new company, and some of them will be good. I think the age of the individual self-publisher seems to be dying. I seem to be one of the last ones and I'm going to be gone in 2007. I don't see anyone coming along; I don't see any new self-publishing wave behind me. And today's comic book business is difficult for the lone wolf because of Diamond's criteria now. It's all different than it used to be. I started in an age of acceptance, now it's a tough business. You know, comics is just like high school. There's a ton of people in it and the ones who stand out are the individuals. They kinda make a name for themselves before the first school year is over – just like in comics. The ones who make a name for themselves are the ones who are interesting to check out; there's something there. There's also a lot of sleepers out there – really cool people who are flying under the radar, and part of the fun of being a comics fan is finding out who the sleepers are, and where the really good stuff is that will make you think, smile and laugh and cry and all that. There's a lot of them out there. That's why reading indy comics is important.

TOUGH LOVE
High School Confidential

Abby
Denson

Excerpted from the forthcoming graphic novel,
"Tough Love: High School Confidential", written and
illustrated by Abby Denson (www.abbycomix.com),
in stores everywhere June 2006 and available
from Manic D Press (www.manicdpress.com)

Excerpted from the forthcoming graphic novel,
"Tough Love: High School Confidential", written and
illustrated by Abby Denson (www.abbycomix.com),
in stores everywhere June 2006 and available
from Manic D Press (www.manicdpress.com)

Excerpted from the forthcoming graphic novel,
"Tough Love: High School Confidential", written and
illustrated by Abby Denson (www.abbycomix.com),
in stores everywhere June 2006 and available
from Manic D Press (www.manicdpress.com)

Excerpted from the forthcoming graphic novel,
"Tough Love: High School Confidential", written and
illustrated by Abby Denson (www.abbycomix.com),
in stores everywhere June 2006 and available
from Manic D Press (www.manicdpress.com)

Excerpted from the forthcoming graphic novel,
"Tough Love: High School Confidential", written and
illustrated by Abby Denson (www.abbycomix.com),
in stores everywhere June 2006 and available
from Manic D Press (www.manicdpress.com)

Excerpted from the forthcoming graphic novel,
"Tough Love: High School Confidential", written and
illustrated by Abby Denson (www.abbycomix.com),
in stores everywhere June 2006 and available
from Manic D Press (www.manicdpress.com)

Excerpted from the forthcoming graphic novel,
"Tough Love: High School Confidential", written and
illustrated by Abby Denson (www.abbycomix.com),
in stores everywhere June 2006 and available
from Manic D Press (www.manicdpress.com)

From an upcoming issue of THE ENCHANTERS. © Steven Gellman

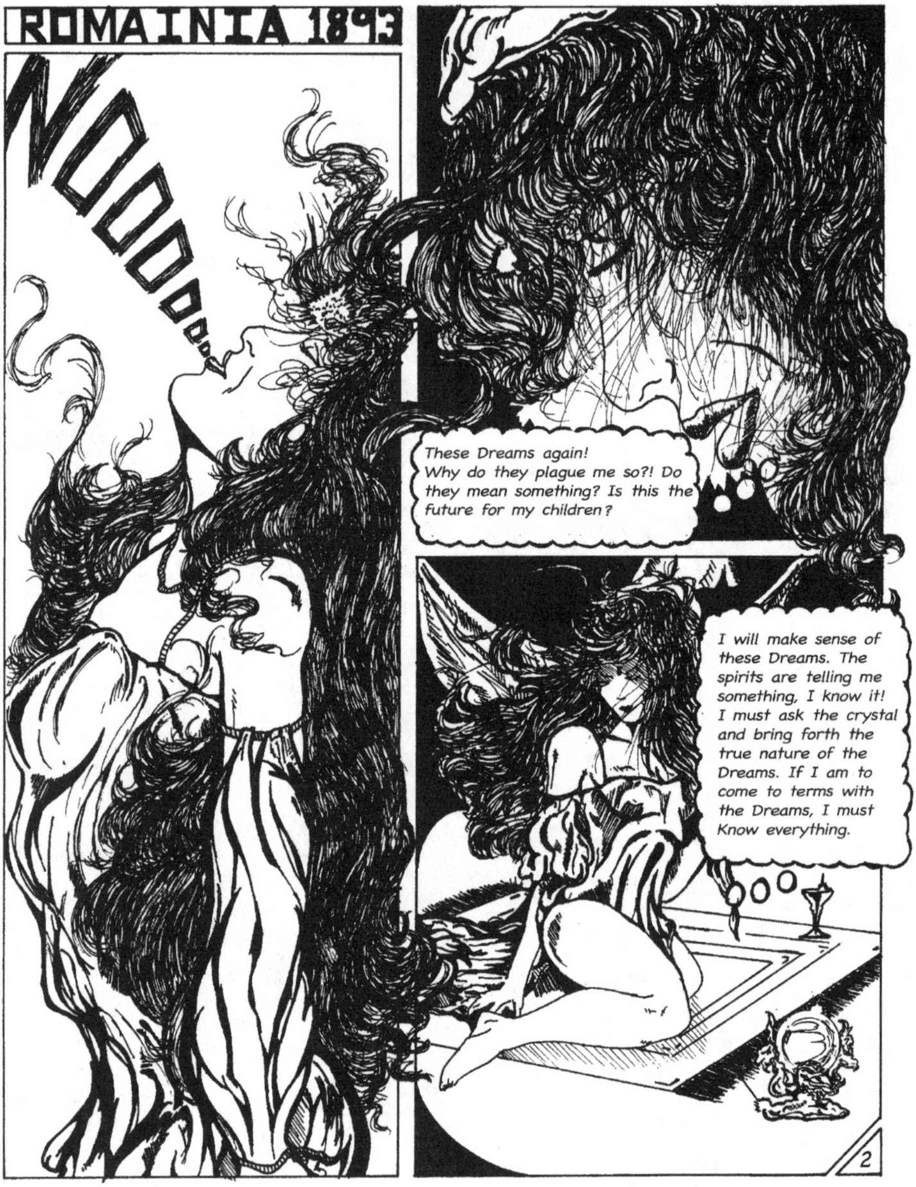
ROMAINIA 1893
NOOOOOOO
These Dreams again!
Why do they plague me so?! Do they mean something? Is this the future for my children?
I will make sense of these Dreams. The spirits are telling me something, I know it! I must ask the crystal and bring forth the true nature of the Dreams. If I am to come to terms with the Dreams, I must Know everything.
2

From an upcoming issue of THE ENCHANTERS. © Steven Gellman

From an upcoming issue of THE ENCHANTERS. © Steven Gellman

Written, illustrated, and © by Justin Hall

Written, illustrated, and © by Justin Hall

Written, illustrated, and © by Justin Hall

Written, illustrated, and © by Justin Hall

YOU **WORSHIP** US DAILY, BUT YOU DON'T KNOW IT.

WHEN YOU GET THE CALL FOR AN INTERVIEW, YOU ASK **US** WHICH TIE MATCHES YOUR SKIN TONE.

WHEN SHE SAYS 'YES', YOU'RE GLAD YOU TOOK OUR **ADVICE** ABOUT JOINING A GYM.

WE'VE ALWAYS BEEN **AHEAD** OF THE CROWD...

...BUT VERY RARELY A **PART** OF IT.

THINGS ARE MUCH BETTER **NOW**, UNDENIABLY.

OUR MUSIC IS PLAYED IN ALL THE BEST CLUBS.

A FAR CRY FROM 'DISCO SUCKS'.

GUYS TAKE BETTER **CARE** OF THEMSELVES.

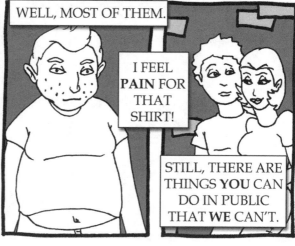

WELL, MOST OF THEM.

I FEEL **PAIN** FOR THAT SHIRT!

STILL, THERE ARE THINGS **YOU** CAN DO IN PUBLIC THAT **WE** CAN'T.

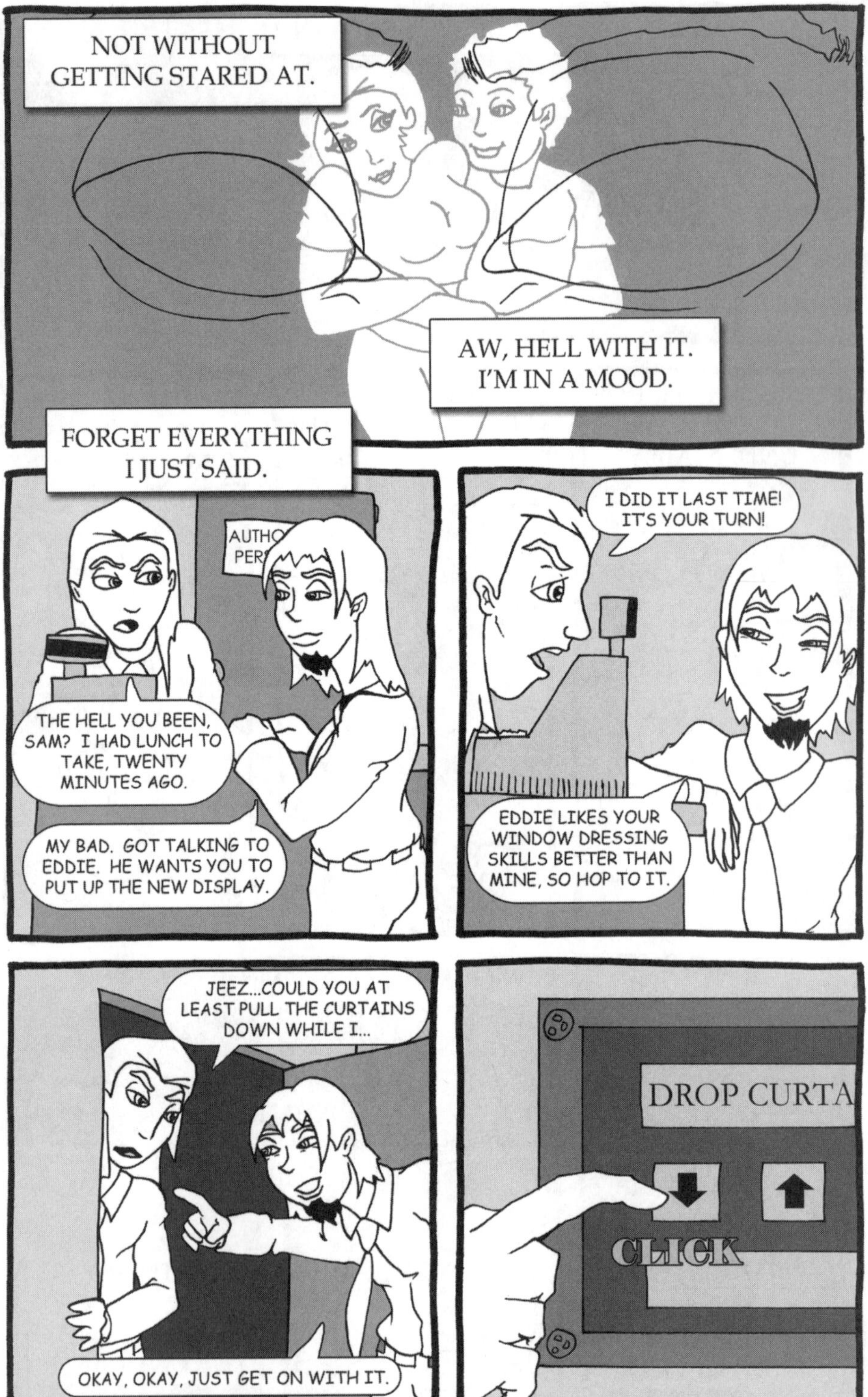
NOT WITHOUT GETTING STARED AT.
AW, HELL WITH IT. I'M IN A MOOD.
FORGET EVERYTHING I JUST SAID.
THE HELL YOU BEEN, SAM? I HAD LUNCH TO TAKE, TWENTY MINUTES AGO.
MY BAD. GOT TALKING TO EDDIE. HE WANTS YOU TO PUT UP THE NEW DISPLAY.
I DID IT LAST TIME! IT'S YOUR TURN!
EDDIE LIKES YOUR WINDOW DRESSING SKILLS BETTER THAN MINE, SO HOP TO IT.
JEEZ...COULD YOU AT LEAST PULL THE CURTAINS DOWN WHILE I...
OKAY, OKAY, JUST GET ON WITH IT.
DROP CURTA
CLICK

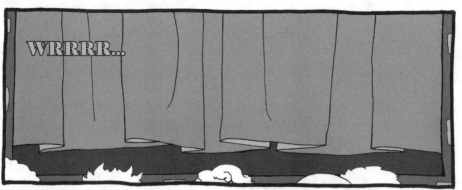

HE'S IN FASHION   STORY: JOHN-PAUL KAMATH   ART: LYNX DELIRIUM

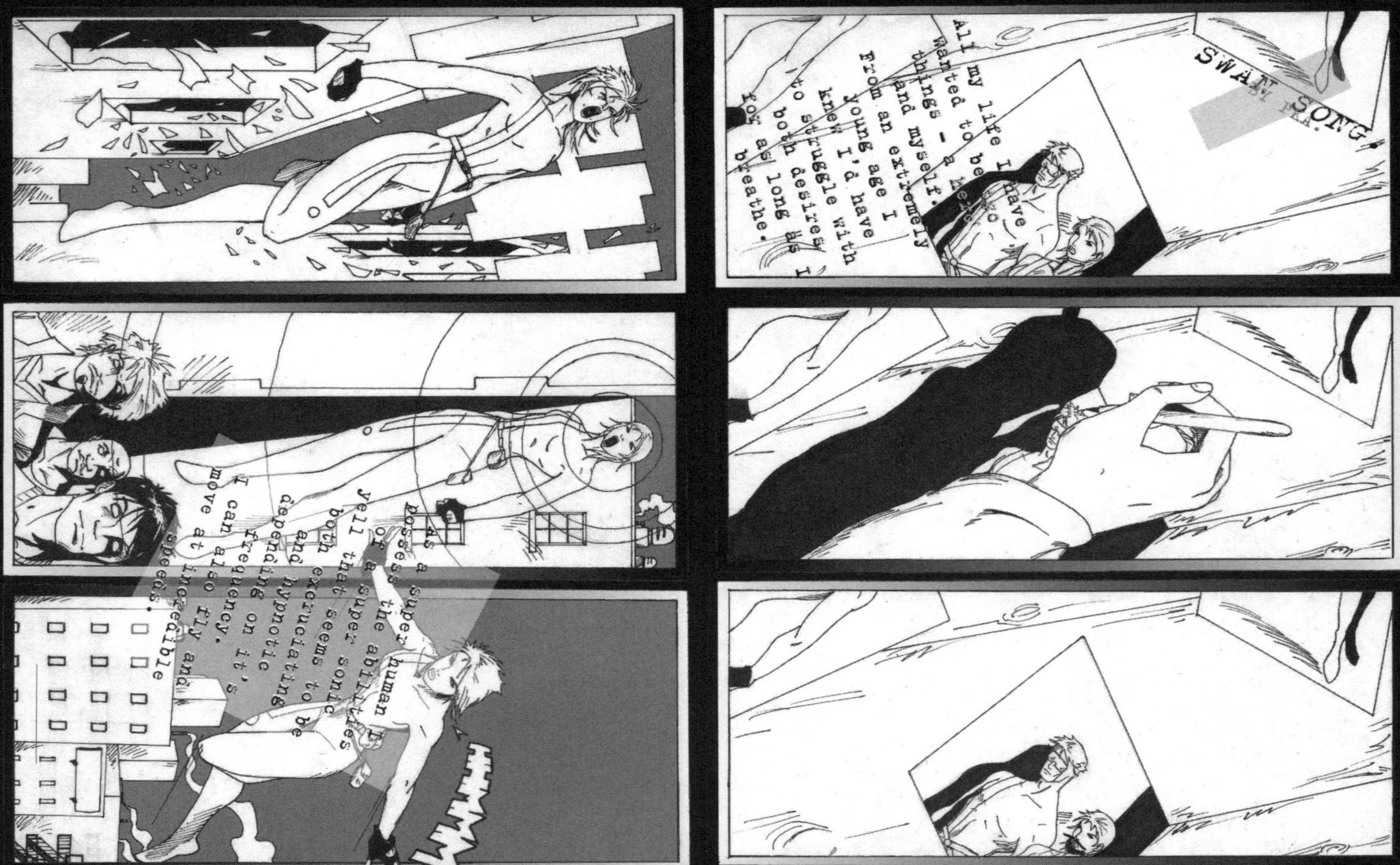
SWAN SONG
All my life I have wanted to be two things – a hero and myself. From an extremely young age I knew I'd have to struggle with both desires for as long as I breathe.
As a super human I possess the abilities of a super sonic yell that seems to be both excruciating and hypnotic depending on it's frequency. I can also fly and move at incredible speeds.

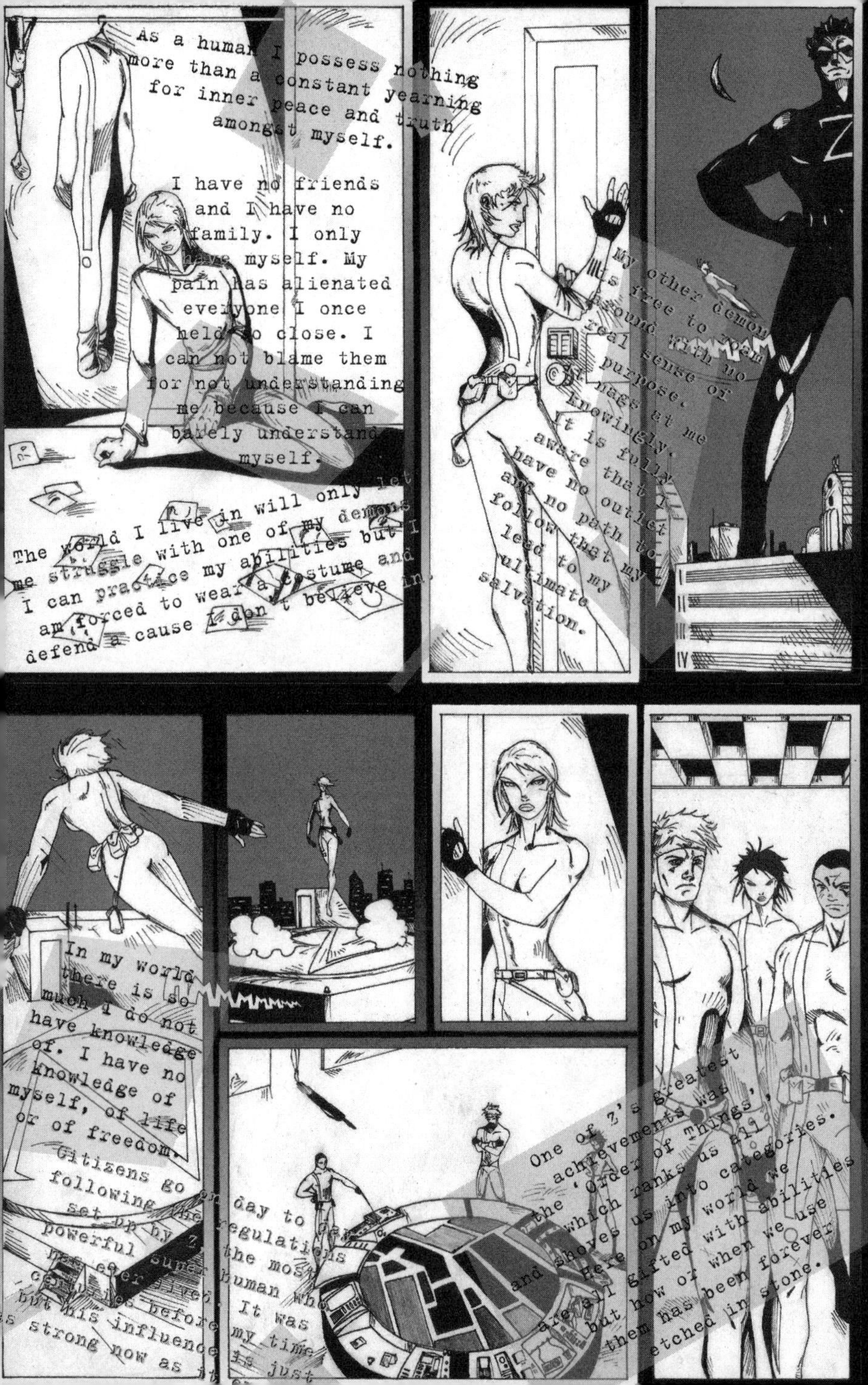

As a human I possess nothing more than a constant yearning for inner peace and truth amongst myself.
I have no friends and I have no family. I only have myself. My pain has alienated everyone I once held so close. I can not blame them for not understanding me because I can barely understand myself.
The world I live in will only let me struggle with one of my demons. I can practice my abilities but I am forced to wear a costume and defend a cause I don't believe in.
My other demon is free to roam around with no real sense of purpose. It nags at me knowingly. It is fully aware that I have no outlet and no path to follow that may lead to my ultimate salvation.
In my world there is so much I do not have knowledge of. I have no knowledge of myself, of life or of freedom.
Citizens go on day to day following the regulations set up by Z the most powerful super human who has ever lived. It was centuries before my time but his influence is just as strong now as it
One of Z's greatest achievements was the 'Order of Things', which ranks us all and shoves us into categories. Here on my world we are all gifted with abilities but how of when we use them has been forever etched in stone.

He never knew his biological parents, some say it's because he never had any. It's not hard to see why one so powerful as Z is speculated to be a product of master gene engineering. Regardless the stories his life was graced by pain at a very early age.

Z was kidnapped when he was only nine years old for a reason that still remains unknown. He was able to escape his captors with ease but upon his arrival home he found his adoptive family slain. He immediately returned to his captors knowing they were responsible and took their lives without hesitation. The world would not hear or see from him for approximately twenty years.

Once Z resurfaced it was only a matter of months before him and his ghost would end up owning us all.

I often find myself wondering a pointless thought - would things be any different today if Z had grown up happy, free of pain. There was no doubt he must have been loved during the few short years he spent with his adoptive family but he grew up so bitter and cold hating all those around him.

He never lost sight of trust though because his advisory was always full of faces. I highly suspect he enjoyed the company but hated the evil capacity we as super humans can and do hold in our hearts.

Our current patrol officer was once on the advisory but was demoted after rumors about his sexuality began to circulate amongst the others. He denied it of course but his words did not hold up against those of his ex-lover who still remains on the advisory.

Despite all these years of trust, I still know next to nothing about the other two members of the patrol. She and I have spoken especially the girl and she appears to have a hidden wisdom, she claims to be from another dimension but I prefer to differ.

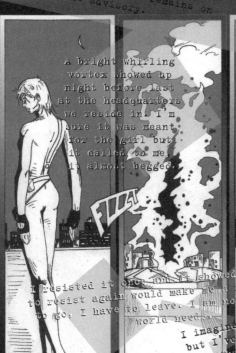

A bright whirling vortex showed up night before last at the headquarters we reside in. I'm sure it was meant for the girl but it called to me, it almost begged.

FIZZT

I resisted it once and it showed once more to resist again would make me a fool. I have to go. I have to leave. I am not what this world needs.

I imagine none of us are strangers to pain but I've got a chance to change things, to perhaps find my ultimate salvation. I believe I'll miss them but I'm too hopeful to care.

"The Anniversary" Preview © Sara Rojo Pérez and Lawrence Schimel. From the forthcoming anthology JUICY MOTHER 2: HOW THEY MET, edited by Jennifer Camper. Published by Soft Skull Press, ISBN 1933368136, US SRP: $ 10.95 US

"The Anniversary" Preview © Sara Rojo Pérez and Lawrence Schimel. From the forthcoming anthology JUICY MOTHER 2: HOW THEY MET, edited by Jennifer Camper. Published by Soft Skull Press, ISBN 1933368136, US SRP: $ 10.95 US

"The Anniversary" Preview © Sara Rojo Pérez and Lawrence Schimel. From the forthcoming anthology JUICY MOTHER 2: HOW THEY MET, edited by Jennifer Camper. Published by Soft Skull Press, ISBN 1933368136, US SRP: $ 10.95 US

"The Anniversary" Preview © Sara Rojo Pérez and Lawrence Schimel. From the forthcoming anthology JUICY MOTHER 2: HOW THEY MET, edited by Jennifer Camper. Published by Soft Skull Press, ISBN 1933368136, US SRP: $ 10.95 US

"The Anniversary" Preview © Sara Rojo Pérez and Lawrence Schimel. From the forthcoming anthology JUICY MOTHER 2: HOW THEY MET, edited by Jennifer Camper. Published by Soft Skull Press, ISBN 1933368136, US SRP: $ 10.95 US

"The Anniversary" Preview © Sara Rojo Pérez and Lawrence Schimel. From the forthcoming anthology JUICY MOTHER 2: HOW THEY MET, edited by Jennifer Camper. Published by Soft Skull Press, ISBN 1933368136, US SRP: $ 10.95 US

EX MACHINA

SPECIAL ADVISORS HAVE A GREAT DEGREE OF LATITUDE, SIR. IT'S IN MY JOB DESCRIPTION.

ANYWAY, MR. WYLIE'S *BROTHER* WANTS THE MAYOR TO PERFORM HIS WEDDING CEREMONY.

OHH, NO! THE LAST THING ANY OF US NEEDS RIGHT NOW IS ANOTHER *WEDDING.*

HOLD ON, YOUR BROTHER THE *FIRE-FIGHTER?* THAT'S GREAT, DAVE!

YOU KNOW I PROMISED EVERY RESCUE WORKER I'D DO WHATEVER I COULD FOR THEM AFTER...AH...

WHAT I MEAN IS, THOSE ARE THE ONLY MARRIAGES I *DON'T* MIND OFFICIATING.

WELL, YOU *CAN'T* DO THIS ONE, SIR.

WHY THE HELL NOT?

BECAUSE MY BROTHER WANTS TO MARRY HIS *BOYFRIEND.*

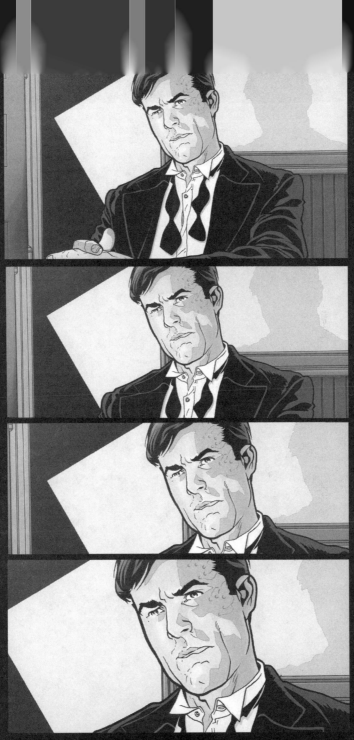

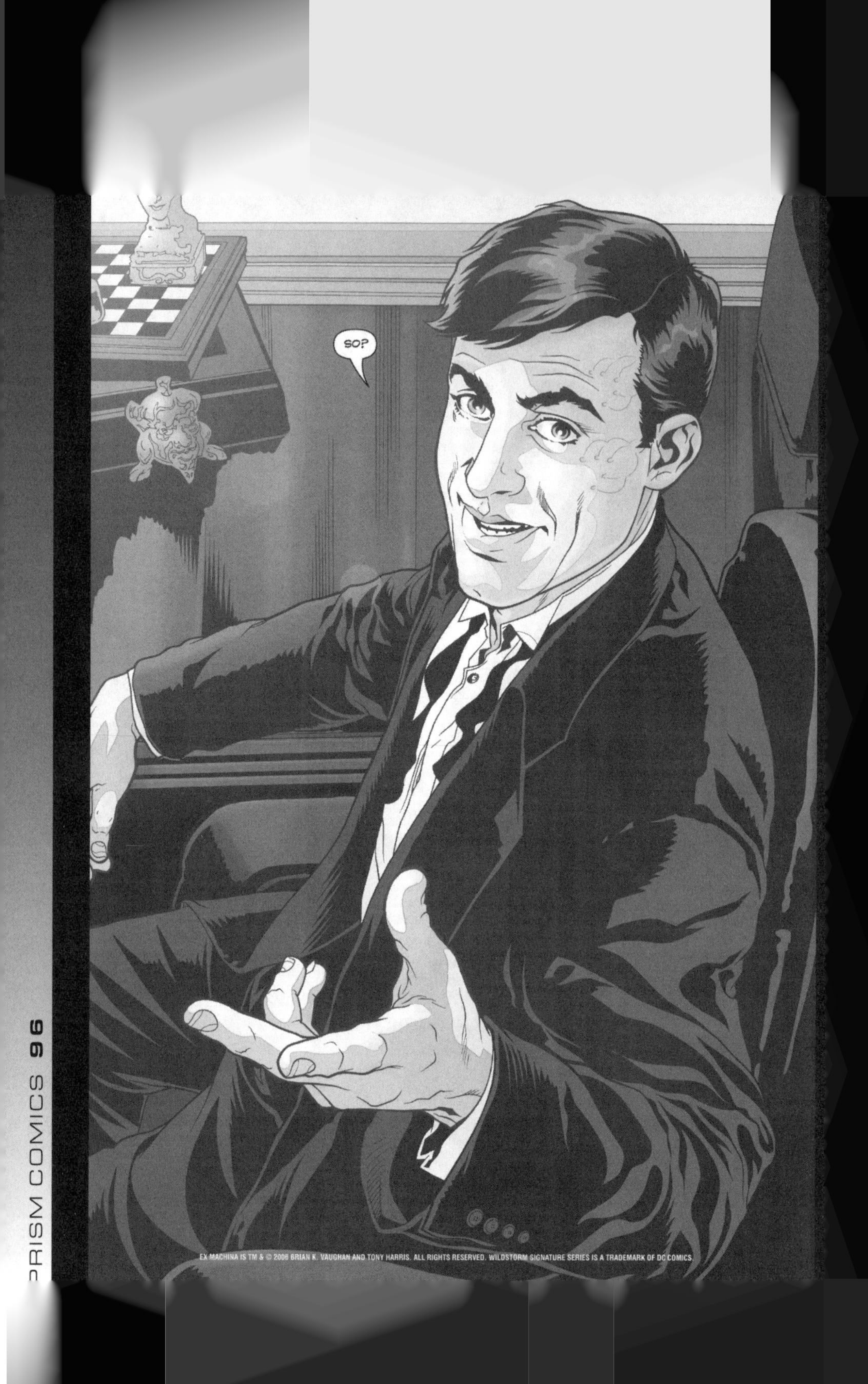
SO?

SCREW THE POLLS.

TUESDAY, MARCH 26, 2002

THIS ISN'T ABOUT DOING WHAT'S POPULAR, DAVE, IT'S ABOUT DOING WHAT'S *RIGHT.*

IT'S NOT ABOUT *EITHER* OF THOSE THINGS, MAYOR HUNDRED! IT'S ABOUT MY KID BROTHER AND HIS OBNOXIOUS BOYFRIEND WANTING TO HAVE A *PARTY* AT GRACIE MANSION.

I HAVE TO SIDE WITH YOUR DEPUTY, SIR. YOU *CAN'T* PERFORM THIS WEDDING. *LITERALLY!* SAME-SEX MARRIAGE IS AGAINST THE LAW IN THE STATE OF NEW YORK... ISN'T IT?

YOU KNOW WHAT ELSE IS AGAINST THE LAW IN THE STATE OF NEW YORK, CANDY? SHAKING A DUST MOP OUT A WINDOW. THAT'S IN THE *BOOKS.*

SHOULD I CALL IN A STRIKE TEAM TO APPREHEND OUR *CLEANING STAFF?*

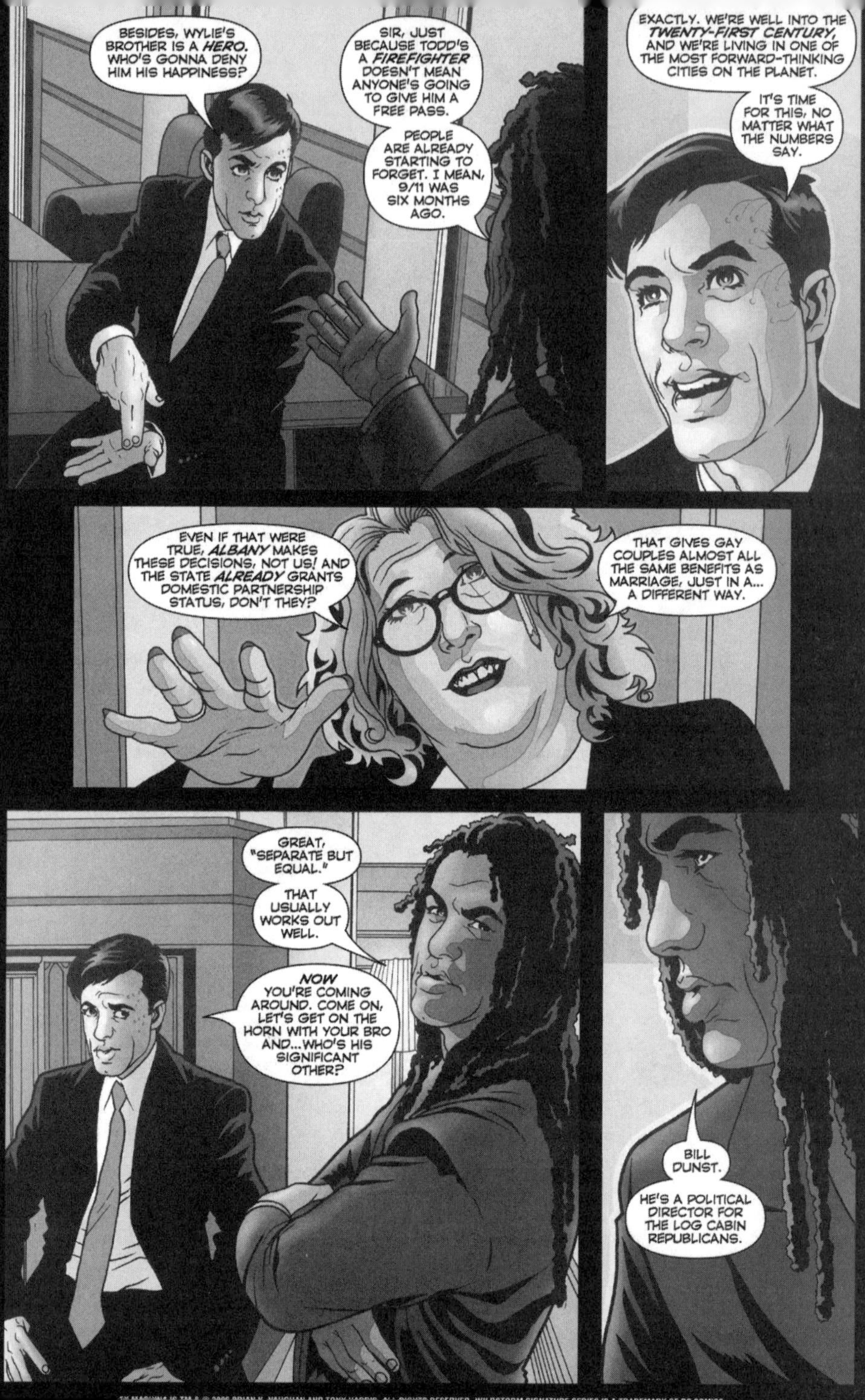

BESIDES, WYLIE'S BROTHER IS A *HERO.* WHO'S GONNA DENY HIM HIS HAPPINESS?
SIR, JUST BECAUSE TODD'S A *FIREFIGHTER* DOESN'T MEAN ANYONE'S GOING TO GIVE HIM A FREE PASS.
PEOPLE ARE ALREADY STARTING TO FORGET. I MEAN, 9/11 WAS SIX MONTHS AGO.
EXACTLY. WE'RE WELL INTO THE *TWENTY-FIRST CENTURY,* AND WE'RE LIVING IN ONE OF THE MOST FORWARD-THINKING CITIES ON THE PLANET.
IT'S TIME FOR THIS, NO MATTER WHAT THE NUMBERS SAY.
EVEN IF THAT WERE TRUE, *ALBANY* MAKES THESE DECISIONS, NOT US! AND THE STATE *ALREADY* GRANTS DOMESTIC PARTNERSHIP STATUS, DON'T THEY?
THAT GIVES GAY COUPLES ALMOST ALL THE SAME BENEFITS AS MARRIAGE, JUST IN A... A DIFFERENT WAY.
GREAT, "SEPARATE BUT EQUAL."
THAT USUALLY WORKS OUT WELL.
NOW YOU'RE COMING AROUND. COME ON, LET'S GET ON THE HORN WITH YOUR BRO AND...WHO'S HIS SIGNIFICANT OTHER?
BILL DUNST.
HE'S A POLITICAL DIRECTOR FOR THE LOG CABIN REPUBLICANS.

PROFILES

Explore a wealth of comics talent with this sampling of the over 180 fantastic LGBT creators (and counting) you can find at **prismcomics.org**. The web site features a lot more art samples, web links and other information. Visit today!

Nathan Aaron
www.nathanaaron.com, www.luxeillustrato.com

Nathan Aaron is an artist who enjoys taking inspiration from the introspective side of life.

He attended the Joe Kubert School of Cartooning and Graphic Art from 1989-92. Moving to Florida, Nathan created STIGMA, an editorial cartoon he wrote and illustrated for two years which won the 1994 Florida Press Association Better Weekly Editorial Award. He also has had the distinguished pleasure of working with New York dance/house musicians Vanessa Daou and Joi Cardwell, designing previous incarnations of their websites as well as an online comic strip based on Vanessa Daou's CD, Plutonium Glow.

After a long stint in graphic design, he has decided to come full circle and immerse himself back into comic book illustration. Nathan is currently working on his upcoming first independent graphic novel, POPLAR. He also completed RAW IN REPETITION originally as an entry for the SPX 2004 Anthology; It didn't make the final cut, but was a great learning experience, and gave it out as a mini comic at the con. You can check out his submission at his website. He also continues to work on his own exhibitions and commissioned works, using a mixture of illustration and watercolor.

Yamila Abraham
www.yaoipress.com

Yamila Abraham is the Managing Editor of Yaoi Press, a lesbian-owned publisher of original English language yaoi graphic novels. Yaoi Press seeks to produce original yaoi manga of the highest caliber and published six books in 2005 alone. Yaoi Press tailors its books specifically for Western audiences, and strives to create titles that appeal to both women and homosexual men. In 2006 Yaoi Press will partner with a major video game company and create at least one yaoi video game.

Yaoi Press is always looking for new talent.

Roberto Aguirre-Sacasa

Roberto Aguirre-Sacasa writes the monthly adventures of the **FANTASTIC FOUR** and **NIGHTCRAWLER** for Marvel Comics and is developing a cartoon series for Nickelodeon, **Punk Rock Angel Girl,** in collaboration with the singer/songwriter Jewel.

His first notable play, **Archie's Weird Fantasy**, explored what would happen if the characters in Archie grew up and were gay. The play was was subsequently re-worked, re-titled to **Golden Age**, and included in the Rattlestick Playwrights Theatre's 2003 Exposure Festival in New York City. Roberto's other successful plays include his Shakespearean romance **Rough Magic**, which transplants characters from **The Tempest** to present-day Manhattan; **The Mystery Plays,** which received the 2002 Roger

L. Stevens Award from the Kennedy Center Fund for New American Plays and in 2004 traveled England as part of the Old Vic/New Voices series; his folkloric thriller **The Muckle Man,** part of Public Theatre's 2002 NEW WORK NOW! Festival; and the occult romantic comedy **Say You Love Satan.**, a runaway hit at the 2003 International Fringe Festival in New York City. **Dark Matters**, his play about the mysteries of deep space and alien abduction, was developed at the 2003 O'Neill Playwrights Conference in Waterford, Connecticut, and presented as a staged reading. It was further workshopped at the Dallas Theatre Center in November of 2003 and the Geva Theatre in Rochester, New York, in March of 2004.

Roberto received his BA from Georgetown University and an MA in English literature from McGill University in Montreal, Canada.

Citizen Rahne Alexander

www.xantippe.com/tranzilla.shtml

Citizen Rahne Alexander is a songwriter & comic performance artist from Baltimore. She is a member of Baltimore's revolutionary queer cabaret, the Charm City Kitty Club, which received a Lesbian Theater Award in 2004 from **Curve Magazine**.

Citizen Rahne's performances have been featured at events from coast to coast, including Baltimore Pride, Gender Crash, Dark Odyssey, the Cinekink Film Festival and Trans-Unity.

2005 was a very productive year for Citizen Rahne. She recorded and released her debut CD, **Blonde On A Bum Trip**. She collaborated on a multimedia performance with media artist Kristen Anchor for the 2005 Transmodern Age performance art festival, and she went on tour of the Mid-Atlantic region with the Tranny Roadshow. Her new garage rock band, the Degenerettes, has also surfaced in Baltimore's underground.

Citizen Rahne is the author of **Tranzilla!**, a self-published zine-style comic book series about a disaffected trannygirl whose rage and tainted hormones turn her into a fire-breathing reptile.

Her writing has appeared in **Radar Review**, **Scarlet Letters**, **Baltimore Gay Life**, and **Manifesto:**. In 2002, she was interviewed about her activist history for the UC Santa Cruz oral history project **Out In The Redwoods**.

Paige and Kevin Alexis

www.FairyFabulous.com

Paige, a former member of the thieves' guild met Kevin, a former member of the Munich circus on a routine mission to Germany. The two instantly fell in love and have been inseparable ever since as PKA. They currently reside in New Orleans where they are trying to make a career out of GLBT super hero comics.

Powers include: converting any object's stored potential energy into explosive kinetic energy and teleportation. Paige prefers to use a deck of playing cards as weapon of choice while Kevin is extremely agile and athletic.

Comics: Currently in print is **ANGLE** #1 which can be found on comixpress.com. **SPARKLE** #1 is also in the works to be printed and will hopefully be out early 2006 along with the first issues of **PRIDE DIVISION, SUPER GYRLZ, and FREEDOM PHOENIX**.

Site: FairyFabulous.com will eventually be host to hundreds of character profiles and 8 super hero comics that follow the old school genre and tradition of costumed do-gooders out to stop the bad guys but adds a modern twist. Most of the ideas and re-occurring themes will follow everyday life such as politics and queer culture along with original, interesting storylines.

Eventually, most of the characters/titles will interact in one way or another. The creators have gone to great lengths to give depth to the characters and storylines alike. FairyFabulous also offers quite a bit of diversity with the characters which is very enlightening.

Marc Andreyko

Marc Andreyko has been a comics fan all of his life and a comics writer since 1994 with his first published work **THE LOST**, his infamous Harvey-nominated, cult comic series. Marc also worked on the Harvey and Eisner winning **DR. STRANGE: WHAT IS IT THAT DISTURBS YOU, STEPHEN?** with artist and friend P. Craig Russell, for whom he translated the Italian opera **Pagliacci: The Clowns**. Other notable collaborations include a **Spider-Man** tale with Jill Thompson in **MARVEL: SHADOWS & LIGHT** and **TORSO** with Brian Michael Bendis.

Other recent and ongoing comics work include **MANHUNTER** for DC Comics, **CASEFILES: SAM & TWITCH** for McFarlane/Image, and **CASTLEVANIA: THE BELMONT LEGACY** for IDW.

In addition to comics, Marc makes his living as a screenwriter in Los Angeles. Past work include a bio-pic on Armand Hammer and the **Torso** screenplay with Bendis for Miramax.

James Asal

www.adamandandy.com, groups.yahoo.com/group/AdamAndAndy/

James Asal lives in Connecticut with Timothy, his partner of 20 years, and their beagle, Baxter. His comic strip **ADAM & ANDY** debuted on the web on May 15, 1999.

ADAM & ANDY appears weekly on its own web site and is featured in several publications in the US and Europe. The feature is translated into German, Turkish, Swedish, Norwegian, and Polish. Readers can sign up for free email subscription to the strip.

The first **ADAM & ANDY trade paperback** collection was published by Studio 64 in October 2003 and is available direct from AdamAndAndy.com or at bookstores worldwide.

Chayne Avery

www.boymeetshero.com

I have lived in New Mexico, the "land of enchantment," my whole life. I grew up in Roswell and no, I've never been abducted by aliens–that I know of! I attended college at ENMU Portales and settled in Albuquerque after graduation in 1995 where I currently own a home with my life-partner, Russell.

I was named after the western movie "Shane." My parents decided to change the spelling to have my name start with a "C," though it's still pronounced "Shane."

In 2000 Russ and I met Jason and Jona Kottler and created a four-issue comic book mini-series called **THE WONDERVERSE**. In 2001, the four of us attended the San Diego Comic-Con and our work was well received for being an unknown, independent title.

My inspiration for **BOY MEETS HERO** comes from all the super hero comic book characters who have a separate and secret romance in their normal lives. Spider-Man has Mary Jane, Superman has Lois. Dealing with protecting a secret identity for the sake of a loved one has been a common theme for these characters for years. One day I wondered, "what if a super hero had a same-sex romance?" That hero would not only have one secret to protect, but also the added pressure of keeping his sexual orientation a secret. So I decided to create the tale of a hero who had these two secrets to protect, and thus, **BOY MEETS HERO** was born!

The basic focus of **BOY MEETS HERO** is the positive relationship that Blue Comet has with his boyfriend, Justin, the people in their lives, and the ups and downs they experience along the way.

Ismael Álvarez (see pages 34, 36)

www.ismaelalvarez.com

My name is Ismael Álvarez. I was born in May 12, 1978 (a Taurus) in Ayamonte, a little village in Huelva, Andalucia, Spain. (Although I'd call it a **big town** now, due to its increasing population…) I am the son of a couple who married young when she was 15 and he 17. A year later I came to life, **SuperIsmael**, ha ha.

Even though it's true that a pencil has never been far from my hand since I was very small, it was only here in Madrid that I developed my work as a comic illustrator, designer and artist. I adore the world of comics in general, the world of eroticism, and—why not say it—the world of pornography. I am one of those who think that it **is** art, whatever way you look at it; I don't believe that the mere act of watching how people perform sex can be considered as something **deviant** and **dirty**. Quite the contrary. At my web site, you will see that I don't beat about the bush; when it comes to illustrating, I do what I want when I want, and if you don't like it, don't look at it.

Sex is beautiful, dear people. Let's look at it the way it is…

Neil Babra

www.neilcomics.com

I'm a cartoonist & illustrator (among other things) from Pennsylvania, now working and residing in the San Francisco Bay Area.

My work has been seen in the **FLIGHT Volume 1** and **Volume 2** anthologies (from Image comics and forthcoming from Random House), **YOU AIN'T NO DANCER**, *Nickelodeon Magazine* and others.

Theo Bain

www.theobain.com, www.britdoodz.com

My name's Theo Bain. I'm from the UK and have been a freelance artist since July of 2003.

I guess its safe to say that Glen Keane is responsible for my desire to work as an artist and illustrator. Ariel the mermaid took my breath away in the Disney animated movie *The Little Mermaid* back in 1989 and I knew from that moment on I wanted to draw for a living.

In 2002 while working in a bookstore, I worked on character designs and story development for an animated project called "Kukani" for Massive Entertainment. To date this project has not gone further than the design stages. In 2003 I got the opportunity to illustrate a comic, which meant I decided to take the leap from fulltime bookseller to fulltime freelance artist.

Being comic artists and fans of the likes of Tom of Finland and Harry Bush, my partner Jack and I saw a big, gaping hole in the UK market for homegrown sexy 'toon guys, so we started BritDoodz.com. We're available freelance for magazine, advertising, promotional stuff, you name it!

I am currently working on a 4 issue miniseries called **THE GIMOLES**, the first issue of available from Alias.

Also, I now illustrate a monthly online comic strip for gaydar.com.

Tim Barela

www.leonardandlarry.com

Native Californian and avid motorcyclist Tim Barela began working professionally as a cartoonist in the mid-'70s. In the '80s, Tim's life and career took a turn out the closet door when he decided to give two minor gay characters from an abandoned project their own comic strip. **LEONARD & LARRY** was enthusiastically accepted by **GAY COMIX**, and made its first appearance in 1984, appearing in several issues, and in a **GAY COMIX SPECIAL**. The strip appeared for many years in the national news magazine **Frontiers**, and was part of ***Out of the Inkwell***, a four-segment play presented in 1994 by San Francisco's Theatre Rhinoceros. **LEONARD & LARRY** has been released in four book collections: **DOMESTICITY ISN'T PRETTY, KURT COBAIN AND MOZART ARE BOTH DEATD, EXCERPTS FROM THE RING CYCLE IN ROYAL ALBERT HALL**, and **HOW REAL MEN DO IT**.

Clive Barker
www.clivebarker.com

Clive Barker was born near Penny Lane, Liverpool, in 1952. He entered Liverpool University to study English literature and philosophy. At the age of 21, he moved to London. There, he formed a theater company to perform plays that he had written, and worked in that medium throughout his twenties as a writer, a director and an actor.

Many of these early plays contained the fantastical, erotic and horrific elements that would later become part of his literary work. They include ***The History of the Devil, Frankenstein in Love***, ***Subtle Bodies***, ***The Secret Life of Cartoons*** and a play about his favorite painter, Goya, entitled ***Colossus***. These works are now seeing publication in the book ***Pandemonium***.

In 1987, following the adaptation of two of his stories for the movies, ***Rawhead Rex*** and ***Transmutations***, (both of which he disliked), he decided to direct something himself.

The result was the first ***Hellraiser* movie**, based on a novella called ***The Hellbound Heart***. The film developed a cult following and has since spawned several sequels, as well as a line of comic books, plastic models and a host of related items.

Barker has also collaborated with his husband David E. Armstrong, a fine art photographer, in his first monograph, **Rare Flesh**, for which he wrote the text. The book is an extraordinary collection of imaginative and sensual male nudes.

Donna Barr
www.stinz.com

Donna Barr has been drawing since 1954, writing since 1963, published since 1986, and publishing since 1996. She has a loyal, eager, world-wide audience for her critically-acclaimed and much-awarded books and series. These include ***The Desert Peach***, ***STINZ***, ***Hader and The Colonel***, and ***Bosom Enemies***.

She is known for her portrayal of male society and hiearchies -- three years in the US Army didn't hurt, there. She has lectured at conventions and symposia all over the United States, Canada and Europe, and is well-known to the growing drawn-book audience in eastern Europe. Her work has been translated into German, Japanese and Italian.

Her website, www.stinz.com, has received praise for its variety, informativeness and ease of navigation. Awards include, the London Comic Creator's Guild's Best Ongoing Humor, Seattle's Cartoonists' Northwest's Toonie, The San Diego Comicon International's Inkpot, and the Washington Press Association's Communicator of Excellence in Fiction.

She is or has been a member of The Graphic Artists Guild, The National Writers Union, and is a consultant for the Media curriculum in the Arts Department at Olympic College, in Bremerton, Washington.

Alison Bechdel
www.dykestowatchoutfor.com

Alison Bechdel's comic strip **DYKES TO WATCH OUT FOR** reproduces the texture of 21st century life, queer and otherwise, in exactingly high resolution. From foreign policy to domestic routine, breastfeeding to chemotherapy, postmodern theory to parenting practice, the finely-drawn characters of **DYKES**

TO WATCH OUT FOR fuse high and low culture in a serial graphic narrative suitable for humanists of all persuasions. **The Comics Journal** says, "Bechdel's art distills the pleasures of **Friends** and **The Nation**; we recognize our world in it, with its sorrows and ironies."

Bechdel grew up in rural Pennsylvania. After graduating from Oberlin College, she moved to New York City, where she began drawing **DYKES TO WATCH OUT FOR** as a feature in the feminist monthly **Womanews** in 1983. Ten book-length **DTWOF** collections have since appeared. Nine of them were published by the pioneering feminist press, Firebrand Books. The most recent volume was released by Alyson Books in the fall of 2003. Other books include **What Do Cats Dream**, **What Do Dogs Dream**, and **Fun Home: A Family Tragicomic**. Her bi-weekly strip is syndicated in over 50 periodicals.

In addition to her comic strip, Bechdel has also done exclusive work for a slew of publications including **Ms.**, **Slate**, **The Village Voice**, **The Advocate**, **Out**, and many other newspapers, web sites, comic books, and 'zines. Her work has been widely anthologized and translated.

Edward Beekman-Myers

cometsweat84@gmail.com

I'm a writer who's been plying the trade in some form or another ever since winning a Young Authors contest in second grade. It only took me 25 years to finally start getting serious about it and try to actually do something with it!

My literary repertoire consists of several short stories (a few of which have been published and a couple of which have won awards), some stage plays (a couple of which have been locally produced), and a series of dark-humored science-fiction novels (which I'm trying to work up the nerve to send out for publication!) I've also had some reviews published in the Queer Eye on Comics series on PrismComics.org. Beyond that, I'm always writing in some form or another, whether it's essays or reviews or just random ramblings.

I do have a few comic book scripts under my belt, and I have a plethora of ideas for many more, but like most newbies, I'm finding it difficult to "break into the biz"—especially since I can't draw or paint worth squat. I'm constantly seeking an artist to team up with to help me bring my visions to life, so if anyone is looking for a partner in four-color crime, give me a holler!

Ken Boesem

www.freewebs.com/barkingraven, www.freewebs.Com/1918

Ken Boesem's short story, "1918," an almost wordless look at how the deadly influenza pandemic of that year circled the globe, appeared in the 2003 **SPX Anthology**. The story was profiled in **Maclean's**, Canada's national newsmagazine.

He has contributed illustrations for many publications including Vancouver's LGBT newspaper **Xtra West** and **Totally Outright: A Guide for Sexual Health Leaders**, a manual targeted at the next generation of young gay men who wish to become sexual health educators.

He is currently working on **THE VILLAGE**, a new bi-weekly comic strip which follows the interwined lives of several colourful characters living and working in Vancouver's gay village in the city's West End.

Fittingly, he lives and works in Vancouver's Davie Village.

Craig Bostick

www.aquaboy.net

Craig Bostick is an illustrator, designer and photographer, working hard to make the world a little easier on the eye. He currently writes and draws **GO-GO GIRL**, an ongoing comic book series about the lighter side of heavy drinking. His other works include **CRASH: THE LIFE AND DEATH OF A GERM, FUCHSIA**

GALACTICA SUMMER SPECIAL and several stories for the 10th anniversary issue of BOY TROUBLE. Most recently he provided the illustrations for the book BAZAAR BIZARRE by Greg Der Ananian published by Viking Studio. He can be found wandering the streets of Boston, Massachusetts, burning the midnight oil at Aquaboy Drawings & Design, or grinding an axe with his band SpoilSport. He married the drummer while attending the 2004 Alternative press Expo and the beat goes onP

Tom Bouden
www.tombouden.be

1971: Tom Bouden is born in Ostend (Belgium).

1980-1982: Tom Bouden decides to become famous. He wants to become a comic artist. Soon the first pages of "Piet & Inge" are drawn. Ten albums are made, varying in length from 4 to 24 pages. The scenarios are often made by friends. Even a "Studio Bouden" is established. Climaxes are the publication of PIET & INGE IN THE JUNGLE in the monthly magazine of a local youthclub and the winning of a comic contest on television.

1983-1988: During high school Tom Bouden is involved in the making of several school magazines and developing new comic characters and series. A few long stories are made. Meanwhile Tom Bouden wins a comic contest in a well-known magazine.

1989-1992: Tom Bouden studies animation in Ghent. He draws many pages involving the medieval figure Boudewijn de Grom. 40 pages out of this collection are later published in an album. In 1990 a gay youth club asks Tom Bouden to make some illustrations for a new campaign. Soon, the figures on the poster (MAX AND SVEN) have leading parts in their own comic. After these stories, Tom Bouden is asked to draw on a regular basis for the monthly Belgian magazine ZiZo. A year later, the Dutch magazine Exprezo follows.

1994: Gags from these magazines are united in the first Tom Bouden graphic album.

1997: Publication in the Dutch Gay-Krant; scripts for Disney Comics and various texts for TV and theatre.

1998: Tom Bouden begins to work as assistant for the famous flemisch newspaper comic FC De Kampioenen.

2000: Publication in the German magazine Queer and Freshmen, the dutch Gay & Night and the English DNA magazine.

2004: MAX AND SVEN is Tom's second book to be published in English. The story, which is a new version of a 1994 comic book, is also published in Dutch, French and Spanish.

Paige Braddock
www.janesworldcomics.com

Hi, I'm Paige Braddock and I'm creator of a comic book titled JANE'S WORLD. For twelve years I worked as a visual journalist for a string of newspapers in the east, including the Chicago Tribune and the Atlanta Journal-Constitution. Even while working in journalism, I spent my free time working on comic concepts, beginning with my youth in the rural South (where there isn't much to do except doodle) and ending in northern California, where I now have the luxury of doing comics full-time.

JANE'S WORLD started out as an online comic and then was picked up for online syndication by United Media for their Comics.com site. After two years of online syndication I decided to make a move to print and published the first Jane comic book at the end of 2002. JANE'S WORLD collections are now available at Borders Books.

This past year Jane was published in French and Spanish… oh yeah, and one 24 page book in Swedish. For more information about our foreign publishers and other news, visit our website.

Jennie Breeden

www.thedevilspanties.com, www.geebasonparade.com

Jennie went to the Savannah College of Art and Design and majored in comics. She's currently 25 and working as a register monkey at Oxford Comics in Atlanta, Georgia. Her web comics work includes **GEEBAS ON PARADE** and **THE DEVIL'S PANTIES**, and she has been a guest at Techwood Con, MomoCon, and Conbust.

Mark Brill

www.markbrill.com

My only real claim to fame thus far is doing card art for *Magic: The Gathering*, *Harry Potter* and the new *Hecatomb* game for Wizards of the Coast. Oh, I did some inking and cover work for Malibu Comics (including four cover paintings for DEEP SPACE NINE) and assorted small publishers including the elusive **PLATYPUS REX** book of my own, not ot mention three gay-rotic comics published under my "furry" psuedonym.

Now, in addition to continuing to produce card game and on-line game art, I'm ready to persue a career doing gay oriented mainstream comics! I'll just mention two projects that I'm currently working on that illustrate this goal:

One is a graphic novel called **THE SUIT**, a dark and surreal story of love, hate and revenge, all of which revolves around a coveted "superhero" costume. This dark tale is written with savage and delightful intensity by a gifted young writer named: Clayton Kinnelon Greiman.

The other is an open-ended (pardon the expression) series called **MARK OF AEACUS** in collaboration with well-known Prism personality and eloquent scribe Charles "Zan" Christensen. **AEACUS** is a hard-edged supernatural thrill-ride of a comic with hot male action on nearly every page! All tastefully done, of course…

With luck and a bit of pressure by the writers…these two comics will be making their debuts in the coming year!

David Paul Brown

www.carabossecomics.com

David Paul Brown is Vice President of Lynx Delirium's Carabosse Comics. In addition to handling most of the business side of the company and working as Lynx's assistant, he was the inspiration for the character Ratboy, who has become one of Carabosse's most popular creations. In an ironic twist, David fashioned a costume based on the Ratboy character and is now the official Ratboy model, posing and making appearances at the Carabosse Comics table at conventions.

David has also done some editing for Carabosse Comics and hand-lettered the one-shot **THE GOTH QUEEN NEEDS A MATE** with an original font he created.

Michael Buzzelli

www.mikebuzzelli.com, www.warpton.com

Mike Buzzelli is a screenwriter, story editor and stand up comedian. He has optioned two feature screen-plays—both comedies—to independent production companies.

His comic book **NORMAL** will be published by Warpton Comics in the United Kingdom later this year. The four issue miniseries features teens who overcome adversity with the help of their unique gifts.

Mike has been honored with awards from the Venice Arts Screenwriting Competition, America's Best Screenplay Competition, Writer's Digest Competition and the One in Ten Screenplay Competition. He has received other national merits and awards as well. His two reader's theater plays for children have been performed in Norfolk, Virginia.

As a stand up comedian, he performs at The Comedy Store, The Ice House, Masquer's Cabaret and coffee houses throughout Southern California.

Jennifer Camper

www.jennifercamper.com

Jennifer Camper is a cartoonist and graphic artist living in Brooklyn, New York. Her art examines gender, race, sexuality and politics, especially from the viewpoint of a Lebanese-American gay woman.

Her books include **RUDE GIRLS AND DANGEROUS WOMEN**, a collection of her cartoons that mix humor with political commentary, and **subGURLZ** (Cleis Press), a graphic novel following the adventures of three women living in abandoned subway tunnels. Camper is also the editor of, and a contributor to, **JUICY MOTHER** from Soft Skull Press, a comix anthology focusing on the work of women, people of color and queers.

Her comics and illustrations have appeared in magazines, newspapers, comic books and anthologies, and her art has been exhibited in the US and Europe.

David Cantero

www.davidcantero.com

David Cantero Berenguer was born December 29th, 1972, in Cartagena, Murcia, Spain.

He studied at the Royal Academy of Beaux Arts in Liège, Belgium, finishing in 1996. Comic strips and illustration were his main studies, but his career has focused more on cartoon animation, learned from Nic Broca, a famous Belgian artist.

He likes to explore new areas in art, such as comic strips, illustration, design, web design, painting, sculpture, photography, dance, music, theater, cinema, etc…

Rondall Carson

www.becomingblizzard.com

So who is Rondall Carson, you ask? And where and when did his artwork become important and how? Rondall has always enjoyed drawing. In high school, he took the required art class, and found that he had natural and focused talent for drawing. It was Rondall's high school art teacher that gave him the encouragement and idea to draw comic strips. Already a fan of Dik Brown's **HAGAR THE HORRIBLE** and Jim Davis' **GARFIELD**, Rondall loved the idea and began creating his own characters.

However, it wasn't until he was in college that Rondall developed the bear characters; Blizzard, Rufus, BC and Jim. This group of four fun loving furry bears would form the basis of a life-long passion and the creation of an animated comic strip. During college, Rondall struggled with confronting his sexual identity. Being attracted to bigger, hairy men, he thought that he didn't fit the "gay" ideal. Gay men were never hairy, never big, and never straight acting. Then later in life after coming out, a friend told him about the gay sub-culture known as "bears." And in that moment he felt that he and his beloved animated bear characters had come home.

Originally, Rondall's concept for the characters in the series was a "Bear" pop/rock band (think **Josie and the Pussycats**). Now, thematically, we will deal with the social and interpersonal issues Blizzard encounters while dealing with his sexual identity. Again this all done with animated bears so the stories will be light hearted & very funny, with many clever pop culture injections. Think, **Will and Grace** meets **The Wonderful World of Disney** or "The Sci-fi Channel" meets "the Gay Bear culture."

The pop/rock band from the original concept will still be part of the story line, as well as the inclusion of some incredible supporting characters: the bands "regular Joe" manager, Charlie; Amadeus the gay vampire bear; and a bear character based on the devil named, LuciBear.

To learn all about this exciting new addition to our community and to meet those lovable bears visit our website.

Christopher Cerasi

www.dccomics.com

A native New Yorker, Chris has been in publishing since 1996. He is currently an Associate Editor in the Licensed Publishing Division of DC Comics, where he edits the **SMALLVILLE** book and magazine programs, as well as the **DC Comics Encyclopedia** from DK, various young adult **Catwoman** film titles, original **Batman** novels, and the novelization for **Batman Begins**. Before that he worked as an editor in the publishing division of Lucas Licensing on many **Star Wars** titles.

Slight and kittenish, Chris is also a freelance writer who fervently wishes he was Lois Lane.

Aman Chaudhary

aman-about-town.com

Aman Chaudhary is a Los Angeles-based art director and illustrator. His published comic book work includes "Trust In Me" in **DOUBLE IMAGE** #5, and FRIGHTENING CURVES with Antony Johnston.

Aman's enjoyment of "bringing people together" is evident each year at Comic-Con, where he hosts "The Big Gay Dinner" for LGBT comics professionals.

Charles "Zan" Christensen

www.onemanguy.com, www.captainkinetic.com, www.Heroplay.com, www.alterworlds.com

Zan aspires to be a lot of things, and his biggest creative dilemma is usually what to tackle next.

His current project is a slice-of-life comedy/drama called ONE MAN GUY, an unconventional look at a man coming to grips, or rather, **not** coming to grips, with a devastating loss.

The series has long been in development, and recently made its debut as a webcomic in the YOUNG BOTTOMS IN LOVE series on PopImage.

His first foray into comics was in 2001 with CAPTAIN KINETIC, a comic book about a closeted superhero from the forties transplanted to present day Chicago.

The series satirizes the squeaky-clean superhero image of a bygone era while using it to make a dramatic point about public and private personae and the importance of defining one's own morality.

In addition to his comics writing, he's the webmaster of several sites for queers and nerds, such as Heroplay (for superhero roleplaying gamers), AlterWorlds (for gay roleplayers of all kinds) and Comics Utopia (for indie comics creators).

Zan has also had a bit of comics journalism ("Ultimate Marvel Cock-Up!") published in an issue of the UK magazine **Comics Forum.**

His fiancé proposed to him on the back cover of **FINDER** #30, and they are currently watching North America closely and waiting for the best place to tie the knot.

Michael Christopher

www.livedlife.com

Michael Christopher has been creating art in the same-gender loving community since 1990. A native of New Jersey, he started out creating flyers for New York City clubs and soon landed the covers for circuit events such as **LA's ATB (At the Beach) Party** and **DC Black Pride**.

Michael's first monthly strip, **G BOYS**, was featured in **WHASSUP! Magazine**, then he went on to create **THE CLIKQUE** for **CLIKQUE Magazine**.

In 1997, Michael decided to take matters into his own hands and started his own comic series called **LIVING THE LIFE** about three friends, Hank, Andre and Kurtis. Hank is a budding hip-hop producer, Andre is a closeted personal trainer, and Kurtis is a rich kid looking for more than the usual shopping spree!

Michael has written two novels based on the characters from the comic magazine and has just finished a screenplay. He currently resides in the Washington, DC area.

Michael has been featured in **Vibe, Honey, The Advocate, The Washington Blade, The New York Blade, MetroWeekly** and **MetroSource**.

In addition to publishing, Michael has been involved in creating HIV-prevention campaigns with the Department of Health in the District of Columbia and Sacramento and has worked with Sacramento's Golden Rule Services and Boston's Global Protection Corp. Michael is on the planning committee of the Ummah Fund's White Attire Affair HIV-prevention benefit and represented his publication, **The Black Pride Resource Guide**, at the Black Media Roundtable On AIDS last fall held by the Black Aids Institute in Atlanta and has committed to devoting content in the Guide to HIV/AIDS awareness.

Chris Companik

www.HIVnMe.com, giantsizecomicbookshow.com

Chris has drawn comics before he could write, and his two current strips **HIV + Me** and **881 MIDTOWN COURT** are as different as night and day. **HIV + ME** is a monthly syndicated strip as a "how-to" guide to living with HIV. Sometimes controversial, often tasteless, but always irreverent, it began attracting national attention after **POZ Magazine** ran his SLEEPING BEAUTY strip (criticizing the lack of needle exchange programs) and began its national rollout. The strip now appears monthly in **A&U Magazine**.

881 has its roots back in the early '80s when a local bar magazine wanted a serialized "gay Luke & Laura" strip and Chris. being the **General Hospital** fan he is, jumped all over it. It now runs in the British gay comic book anthology **BUDDIES**.

When not doing comics, Chris also produces for Atlanta's People TV, including his monthly series **Giant Size Comic Book Show**. Among other recent productions have been the roundtable discussion show of gay life in Atlanta "**Out Out & Away**" and a series of safe sex spots, including the award-winning "A Condom Will Fit Over a Grapefruit."

Michael Cooke

home.earthlink.net/~mykill23/michael.html

Michael Robin Cooke here. I've been a wannabe comic creator all my life and wax and wane with attempts to go "pro." Otherwise I'm a graphic designer with a lot of production experience. I spent a year at the Joe Kubert School, I write an interesting edgy story and I'm developing a personal digital drawing style.

Published work: ITHACAT was a weekly newspaper strip I wrote and illustrated. PSYCHE VAMPYRES has been published in a small press magazine. **V-MAN** is another small press publication.

Currently I'm developing **SODOMIGHT**, a gay superhero comic... sorta.

I live in New York City with my partner of the past 7 years, Lance.

Colleen Coover (see page 42)
www.livejournal.com/users/colleencoover/

Colleen Coover is the bisexual creator and artist of **SMALL FAVORS**, a girly porno comic for adults. **SMALL FAVORS** tells the story of two women, Annie and Nibbil, who enthusiastically enjoy sexual romps with each other and with several pretty friends. Colleen's happy, funny comics of love and sex have delighted readers of all genders and orientations! **Volume 1** and **Volume 2**, collecting the first seven issues, have been published by Eros Comix, and issue #8, a fully painted color special, is still available. Konkursbuch has published German language translations of the complete series.

Colleen's current project, with writer Root Nibot, is a comic book mini series for all ages, **BANANA SUNDAY**. Featuring the timeless themes of teen romance, teen angst, and talking monkeys, **BANANA SUNDAY** is a lighthearted story of friendship, loyalty, and the challenge of staying awake through a day in high school. The four-issue series is published by Oni Press, with a collected volume scheduled for Spring 2006

Colleen has contributed comic work to *Out* and the anthologies **WHAT RIGHT?** and **TRUE PORN**. She has done illustration and cover design for *On Our Backs*, *Girlfriends, Curve*, *Kitchen Sink Magazine*, *Nickelodeon magazine*, Buckle Down Publishing, Alyson Books, and Cleis Press.

Colleen lives in Portland, Oregon with her boyfriend and creative partner, Paul Tobin (Root Nibot's alter ego). She has no website, but keeps a blog at LiveJournal.com, and can be contacted by email.

Jordan-Mykal Cross
comicbookartistboi@yahoo.com

I have drawn since i was a kid. Did work for Assination Entertainment and went to the Art Institute to get a degree in Computer Animation.

I am a colorist and illustrator for pin-up style art. I also deal in custom comic book doll-making, custom figures, and character design and modeling in 3-D.

I am a Pagan, and so specialize in Goddess and Tarot represenational art. I am also currently working on designs that bridge the gap between anime and comic book style art–a little of both, but neither completely.

Howard Cruse
www.howardcruse.com

Howard Cruse is the creator of **WENDEL**, the 1980s comic strip about a circle of gay friends that was collected in its entirety in 2001 in a book called WENDEL ALL TOGETHER. His 1995 graphic novel, STUCK RUBBER BABY, won both Eisner and Harvey Awards in 1996, and has since won awards in England and Germany. An Italian translation of **SRB** has also been published and Spanish translations of both **SRB** and **WENDEL ALL TOGETHER** are now in production. **STUCK RUBBER BABY**'s French edition won the Prix de la critique at the Angouleme comics festival in 2002. Many of Howard's underground comix were compiled more than a decade ago in the books Early Barefootz and Dancin' Nekkid With the Angels.

Howard's newest book, THE SWIMMER WITH A ROPE IN HIS TEETH, an illustrated adaptation of a fable by Jeanne Shaffer, was published by Prometheus Press in April of 2004. Many of his comic strips, both old and recently drawn, are archived on his extensive website, Howard Cruse Central. Recently completed projects are new comics created for inclusion in future edition's of Jennifer Camper's **JUICY MOTHER** series and a five-page gay webcomic drawn for Tim Fish's YOUNG BOTTOMS IN LOVE. Meanwhile, an array of Howard's drawings are currently decorating tee-shirts, mugs, mouse pads and other cool merchandise at his online merchandise shop, Cruse Goodies, now open for business at CafePress.

Javi Cuho

www.javicuho.tk

Javi Cuho is a young Spanish comics scriptwriter. He was born June 2nd, 1981, in the Mediterranean city of Barcelona and since he was a child, writing has been his passion.

His first comic book, called **NO TE ESPERABA** (with artist Hokane) was recently published in Spain by Odisea Editorial. It's an intense, deep and passionate story where the author relates to us an impossible relationship between two men.

Nowadays, he's working with the great Spanish artist David Cantero on differents comics projects, such as **SIN COMPASIÓN** (Merciless), **VÍCTOR & ÁLEX**, **FALLEN ANGELS**, and much more...

MK Czerwiec

www.comicnurse.com

I am an artist and nurse living in Chicago. I post a cartoon every Monday on my website, ComicNurse. com.

SCARS, STORIES AND OTHER ADVENTURES is my self-published first collection and is available on my web site. My second collection should be ready for puchase later this year.

Among other projects, I am currently working on a graphic memoir of the six years I spent in AIDS care in the early '90s. Not very funny stuff, but it had its moments. My goal is to memorialize and share the stories of some incredible moments I had the privilege to witness there, and remind myself what they taught me.

I also write for Sequential Tart Webzine, so if you're interested in a review or interview, email me.

Dave Davenport

www.dogspunk.com

Dave Davenport is a tattoo artist and illustrator living/working in the Silver Lake/Echo Park area of Los Angeles. His comic work is too smutty for the Xeric award, but has appeared in the Prism Comics anthology UNSAFE FOR ALL AGES as well as in **TRUE PORN 2**.

He self-publishes **DOGSPUNK COMIX** and is scheming with fellow perv Justin Hall to put a book out together. He has also been known to work with writer Steven Lozier.

Darren Davis

www.bluewaterprod.com, www.aliasenterprises.com

Darren Davis was making his way in the world by marketing the entertainment industry at such companies as E! Entertainment Television and USA Networks, when he left to pursue his creative dreams in publishing. He took on a position at Wildstorm Studios, which shortly after joined with comic book conglomerate, DC Comics. After his tenure in corporate America, Darren joined on as President of Joe Madureira's Beyond Entertainment, which publishes such titles as **BATTLE CHASERS**.

Following several years with Wildstorm, Darren took the next step towards creative freedom and formed his own publishing company where he created such popular titles as **10TH MUSE, LEGEND OF ISIS** and **ZAK RAVEN ESQ.**

Darren continues to represent the top comic book talent in the industry while writing comics and novels, and works as Editor-in-Chief for Angel Gate Press.

Sven de Rennes

www.svenderennes.com

I'm working as a cartoonist under the pseudonym of Sven, born in 1971, I'm living in Rennes, Britany (France). I began drawing a few years ago, after completing my studies at the Rennes University of Art.

Initially, my drawings were confined to the themes of fantasy and science fiction, then in March or 2002, I decided to tackle the gay universe. My art deals with situations that are sometimes tender, occasionally astonishing, often funny and frequently exciting.From the cool guy with suggestively snug jeans through the fit lifeguard on the beach to the sexy surfer.

I wish you a good visit and an enjoyable time on my universe.

Adam DeKraker

adamdek@aol.com

Adam DeKraker's pencils have appeared in such popular DC titles as **THE TITANS, ADVENTURES OF SUPERMAN, BIRDS OF PREY,** JSA: ALL STARS, **SECRET FILES, SUPERBOY, LEGIONNAIRES, JSA 80 PAGE GIANT,** and many others. He has inked DC's **SMALLVILLE, CATWOMAN, BATMAN,** and many titles from Nickelodeon Magazines, including *Rugrats, Jimmy Neutron,* and *Danny Phantom.*

Adam has also contributed penciling, inking, and full art to titles from Wildstorm Comics, Marvel Comics, Lonestar Press, Disney Adventures, Wilson Place Comics, Cryptic Press and many other publishers.

He lives in Brooklyn, NY.

Lynx Delirium

www.carabossecomics.com

William Tyler, working under the name Lynx Delirium, has had sequential art and stories showcased in several anthologies including **POTLATCH PROJECT** #4 from Angry Dog Press, Prism Comics' annual guide and Tim Fish's hit webcomic **YOUNG BOTTOMS IN LOVE** at PopImage.com. He self-publishes fantasy stories through his creator-owned company Carabosse Comics. The imprint debuted in 2004 with the one-shot THE GOTH QUEEN NEEDS A MATE which was listed as one of the best indy buzz-books of that year in **Wizard Edge Magazine**.

He is currently working on an ongoing title FAIRIES TELL which is a retelling of classic children's stories, nursery rhymes and fairytales from the point of view of the actual fairies who witnessed them.

In addition, he is constantly working on Lynx's Pinup Boys, a series of illustration art prints focusing on the male form.

Abby Denson

www.abbycomix.com

Abby Denson's gay romance comics, including TOUGH LOVE and POP SECRET, have been running in *XY* magazine since 1996. Other comics she's created include: DOLLTOPIA, NIGHT CLUB, and DEADSY CAT & KISSY KITTY.

She also scripts licensed comics including POWERPUFF GIRLS, THE SIMPSONS, SABRINA THE TEENAGE WITCH, JOSIE AND THE PUSSYCATS, DISNEY ADVENTURES, and comics for *Nickelodeon magazine.*

She rocks out in her spare time with her band The Saturday Night Things. She loves New York, container gardening, and petting her cat, Slinky.

Michael Derry

www.troycomics.com, www.derryproducts.com

Born in Rockford, IL., Michael escaped in the late 80's to Northern Illnois University where he studied illustration and theater. He graduated in 1994 with a BFA in illustration and moved to Chicago to make a name for himself as an illustrator and cartoonist. He instead got cast in several stage productions and after five years of acting and bartending, moved to LA to pursue acting. Again, life threw him a curve and he ended up doing illustration and animation (and more bartending) which lead to the creation of **TROY**.

He has been writing and drawing **TROY** since 1998. In March of 2004, he optioned **TROY** as a live-action feature and possible TV series through Envision Entertainment in Hollywood and is currently working on the the screenplay.

His other work through Derry Products includes magazine and commercial illustration, character design and animation, greeting cards, and storyboards and comps for commercials.

He currently lives in West Hollywood with his partner of over four years. When he's not working (which is rarely these days) he likes to read, lounge in the pool, and throw fabulous cocktail parties complete with maraschino cherries, little cocktail umbrellas, and what his dear friend and sparring partner calls "affordable ambiance".

Peter Di Maso

www.peterwerk.com, www.corridart.com

Peter Di Maso was born and raised in Montreal, where he trained in design and art history. After a five-year stint at the National Gallery of Canada in the early 90s, Peter landed in Los Angeles, where he now works as a webmaster for Advocate.com. Peter is working on a self-published anthology of so-called "counter-autobiographical" comics called **THE ELEGANT FIREFIGHTER**.

Diane DiMassa

www.hotheadpaisan.com

Diane DiMassa is the creator of the comic 'zine **HOTHEAD PAISAN: HOMICIDAL LESBIAN TERRORIST**, which has been appearing quarterly for seven years from Giant Ass Publishing. The first 20 issues have been collected in three volumes. **Hothead Paisan** was also part of *Out of the Inkwell,* a four-segment play presented in 1994 by San Francisco's Theatre Rhinoceros, and DiMassa's work has been featured in **GAY COMICS,** *Strange Looking Exile, Frighten the Horses, The Advocate*, and *Oh...*

Catherine Doherty

www.thejanewaynes.com

Born in Toronto in 1965, Catherine Doherty became interested in comics when she discovered the unpublished work of her father's in a metal file box in the basement. Her first published work appeared in Vancouver's *A Room of One's Own* and London's *Diva* magazine, and she later appeared in Toronto's *Siren,* and in **GAY COMICS**. Her first graphic novel, **CAN OF WORMS**, was published by Fantagraphics Books in 2000 and was nominated for an Eisner Award. It is a thinly veiled autobiographical story about growing up adopted and her search for her birth mother.

Doherty is currently working on her second graphic novel, a biography of a forgotten opera singer. She is also a set/production designer for film and plays banjo in an all-girl Toronto cowboy band called The Jane Waynes.

Jenn Dolari

www.dolari.org/awfw, www.dolari.org/cs

Jenn Dolari has been a comics pusher, cash register slave, Usenet junkie, Mortal Kombat afficionado, video game conceptual artist, tech support guru and web comic publisher (although she had to be fired from most of the above for that last one).

Her comics, **A WISH FOR WINGS** (about a woman's quest to be an angel), and **CLOSETSPACE** (about a boy's quest to be a woman) have been wandering their way around the Internet weekly since 2001.

She spends most of her free time in Austin, Texas, in a blind panic over how she'll manage to get next week's comics done.

Kris Dresen

www.krisdresen.com

Kris Dresen is an artist and writer living in Chicago. She's the illustrator of the critically acclaimed comic book **MANYA**, written by Jen Benka, and the writer and artist of her solo strip, **MAX & LILY**. Previously awarded the Xeric Grant, Kris and Jen were nominated for an Eisner Award for their work on **Manya**.

Outside of comics, Kris is an art director of children's books and freelance illustrator. While she waits for Jen to finish writing the next **MANYA** book, Kris is drawing a graphic novel she's written called **GRACE** that will serialize on her website starting in early 2006. All Kris will say is that **Grace** will have many, many drawings of naked women in it

Jamaica Dyer

www.jamaicad.com

Jamaica has always told stories through pictures and words, from the paper cut-out characters she drew as a little kid to photocopying black and white minicomics and selling them on convention floors as a teen. Her minicomics ranged from early angsty autobio comics to her massive apocalyptic noir comic **ECHOES IN THE ASHES**. In 2004 she worked on the comic **SUICIDE PACT**, self-published by her partner Violet Hemlock. Jamaica's work has appeared in various publications, including **SPARK GENERATORS II**, *Kitchen Sink Magazine*, a future issue of **JUICY MOTHER** and she did a weekly comic strip in the *Spartan Daily* newspaper.

Currently she's attaining a BFA in animation, doing freelance illustration, and working on the next Great American Novel while bald girls with black eyes and pretty boys in skirts dance through her head.

C. Edwards

www.abelboddy.com

C. Edwards forfeited a formal art education so that he could study **NEW TEEN TITANS** comics and classic issues of *Men's Fitness.*

After spending a decade drawing pictures for Cartoon Network and Nickelodeon (among others) and working on the Adult Swim cult hit *Aqua Teen Hunger Force*, he has dedicated the remainder of his art career to drawing whatever the hell he wants. Which begins with his online comic strip ABEL BODDY.

He is inspired by great modern artists like Tom of Finland, Maurice Vellekoop, Jordi LaBanda, Luc LaTulippe, Alan Davis, Chuck Jones and Stephen Sondheim.

C. Edwards can currently be seen walking around the metropolitan area listening to his iPod. He is apathetically single, has no pets and enjoys looking out at the world with a strong sense of bitterness and resentment.

Dylan "NDR" Edwards

www.studiondr.com

Dylan "NDR" Edwards is a writer, artist, and cartoonist currently living in Austin, Texas. His work appears both in print and on the web. His print works include his regular weekly editorial cartoons for **TXT Newsmagazine**, as well as appearances in a variety of queer-themed magazines and newspapers. He has self-published three minicomics to date.

He also appears as a regular monthly cartoon feature on-line at Outsports.com, and presents a wide variety of his cartoons on his own website.

His comic about gay Republicans and their friends and relations, **POLITICALLY INQUEERECT**, is probably his most popular feature. PIQue is scheduled to make a major print appearance in 2006.

Kurt Erichsen

www.kurterichsen.com

Kurt Erichsen has been a widely published gay cartoonist since 1980, with stories in such publications as **GAY COMIX**, **Meatmen**, **Instinct** magazine, **Starlog**, and **Fairy Flicks**. He is the artist and writer of **MURPHY'S MANOR**, the longest running gay syndicated comic strip, since 1982. **MURPHY'S MANOR** twice received awards from the Gay/Lesbian Press Association. In 2002 Kurt received the Rostler Award (the lifetime cartoonist award) from SCIFI Inc.

JC Etheredge

www.anti-heroes.net

I've been drawing all my life. I can't remember when I started but it was early. My earliest influences were Charles Schulz's **PEANUTS**, **Tiny Toons,** and of course, **X-MEN**.

Apparently, it didn't take long for me to start drawing erotic images. The first pornographic thing I ever drew was a nude, erect Eric from the **Little Mermaid**. That came out in 1989, meaning I was nine or ten when I drew it!

I hand draw and ink all my characters and can never be found without a trusty mechanical pencil or micron handy. I like to experiment with a variety of different media for color but for the most part, I use Photoshop.

My goal is to do it all in the field of illustration. I want to have monthly comic books, do character design for games and animation, and of course, change the world with my work! Well, maybe that's taking it too far. As long as I make someone laugh, that's cool with me.

Matt Fagan

www.geocities.com/meniscusenterprises

I have written, drawn and printed the zine **MENISCUS** since 1998, a grab-bag of literary whimsy governed by the motto "a publication dedicated to upholding the rights of the ugly - but not the stupid". The zine has always been peppered with artwork and comics, but in the past few years **MENISCUS** has not been strong enough to contain them all. So, under the umbrella of Meniscus Enterprises, I have produced a number of mini-comics such as **LITTLE GRANDPA**, **TORCH SONG** and **I HAD TO GET A STUPID ROOT CANAL**. The largest undertaking, though, was the 60-page horror-comedy **DOMESTIC PARTNER OF FRANKENSTEIN**, which has received some good notices.

I also illustrate the review zine **Xerography Debt**, edited by Davida Gypsy Breier, and recently completed a series of illustrated conversations for a book edited by Benn Ray of Atomic Books in Baltimore. If you happen to be a fan of America's pastime and live in the Milwaukee area, you might have seen my work on several pages of the current (fourth) issue of **B-FORCE**, a public-service comic published by Marvel in which the Milwaukee Brewers battle the evils of chewing tobacco. That's right, it's real.

Currently, I am working on a series of one-page comics entitled **LOVE**. The serial is about two disenfranchised young gay men (Jack and Pokie) struggling to maintain their foothold in a world that does not seem to have a place for them—not because they're gay, but because they're smart and self-aware. The first one hundred twenty pages have been collected in three volumes, available through my web site as well as Prism Comics' online store.

You can also find my writing in **Thought Magazine**, **Little Engines**, and **McSweeney's**.

Patrick Fillion
www.patrickfillion.com, www.classcomics.com

From the moment he was born, Patrick was an artist. Preferring pencil and paper to most other toys as a child, he would draw for hours on end. As an adult, Patrick's love of art and comics in particular is stronger than ever. Today, he and his life and business partner, Fraz have created their own independent publishing company called Class Comics. Through this company, they produce and print several gay erotic themed comics such as **NAKED JUSTICE**, **CAMILI-CAT** (whom Patrick created 20 years ago, at the age of 12), **SATISFACTION GUARANTEED**, **GUARDIANS OF THE CUBE**, **DEIMOS**, and the anthology series called **RAPTURE**.

Class Comics titles are translated into French by one of France's leading publishers of gay literature, H&O Publications. Their titles are also made available in German by the publisher Bruno Gmunder and if you live in Europe, you can even get your hands on European Editions of the English Class Comics titles, also published by BG. Currently, there are plans to further translate all Class Comics books into Spanish.

2005 was a big year for Patrick. It saw the release of his first two hardcover art books, one released in French and English by H&O called **Boytoons**, and the second entitled **Heroes**, released through Bruno Gmunder. Later in the year, BG released a trade paperback graphic novel entitled **THE INCREDIBLY HUNG ADVENTURES OF THE MIGHTY MALES**, featuring several of Patrick's original characters. And just recently, BG has released a line of desk diaries and 2006 calendars, featuring Patrick's sexy and heroic Boytoons.

2005 also saw Class Comics release their first two full-color comics: **RAPTURE #1** and **GUARDIANS OF THE CUBE #5**. With 2006 on its way, Patrick and his partner have a whole lot of goodies planned, including 6 new full color Class Comics titles, and a new hardcover artbook with Bruno Gmunder entitled **Hot Chocolate**.

When Patrick is not busy writing, drawing and publishing comics, he is hard at work illustrating for several well known gay publications, such as **BLACK INCHES**, **LATIN INCHES** and recently **FRESHMEN** magazine.

Tim Fish
www.timfishworks.com

Tim Fish writes, draws and self publishes a variety of comic book series and one-shots.

His **CAVALCADE OF BOYS** 3-volume trade paperback collection—which made **The Advocate**'s summer reading list—is available nationwide. The collections compile every **CAVALCADE** story ever made. H & O Editions has also published a French translation of **CAVALCADE**.

In addition, Tim is the mastermind behind the defunct daily **YOUNG BOTTOMS IN LOVE** which ran at PopImage.com.

Tim turns to the dark side with an upcoming original graphic novel about (gasp!) straight people.

Greg Fox
www.kylecomics.com

Greg Fox is the creator of **KYLE'S BED & BREAKFAST**, a comic strip about a gay B&B in the suburbs, that is currently running in numerous gay publications across North America, online, at the official **Kyle's Bed & Breakfast** website, and on the *Out In America* cities network of websites. Sexy, addictive, sometimes shocking and laugh-out-loud true, **KYLE'S BED & BREAKFAST** is the ongoing story of a group of neurotic, gorgeous, and always interesting gay men sharing their lives, their ambitions, and one extremely cramped bathroom. Gay newsmagazine *The Advocate* named **KYLE'S BED & BREAKFAST**'s web home as one of their "Hot Websites." It has also been featured in *Genre* and *Instinct* magazine, and also written about in *The New York Times* and in *Newsday*. In late 2004, the first collected edition of **KYLE'S BED & BREAKFAST** was published by Kensington Books. The book was a finalist in the humor category in the 2005 **Lambda Literary Awards**.

Greg has done work for comics publishers as well, including **DOCTOR CHAOS** for Triumphant Comics, and **BASEBALL SUPERSTARS** and **ROCK 'N' ROLL COMICS** for Revolutionary. He did one job for Marvel, **NFL QUARTERBACK CLUB**.

Leanne Franson
liliane.keenspace.com, leannefranson.com

Hullo! My name is Leanne Franson, not to be confused with my main character, also a bi-dyke, whose name is Liliane. Liliane has no nose. I do.

I first started drawing comics in a sketchbook after I finished a degree in Fine Arts at Concordia University in Montreal in 1985. Somehow I decided everything I did should be FINE ART, and thus I did nothing. While working in a coffeeshop (yes, of course, I had a degree in Art!) I quickly got bored with the less-than-amusing comic strips in the daily newspaper and decided my own life was wackier.

Thus LILIANE (since French Canadians seem stymied by "Leanne" and translate it immediately to "Liliane") was born in minimum wage and caffeine. LILIANE reflected the lesbian and bisexual realities of the '90s, as well as being used as a therapy tool by me. It is incredible how much funnier all one's annoyances and horrid memories are once committed to paper with a punchline added.

Following another lover to England, UK LILIANE appeared in 1994, and was quickly picked up by Peter Pavement of the now defunct Slab-O-Concrete, who shoved her out into the great world between the covers of her first two *real books*, **ASSUME NOTHING: EVOLUTION OF A BI-DYKE** in 1997 and **TEACHING THROUGH TRAUMA** in 1999.

The disappearance of Slab coincided with an upswing of my career in children's book illustration, and I laid down my technical pens until late 2003. The sudden revival of LILIANE may be credited to Sue Marsden of ABRAXIA, who commissioned a page in summer 2003, and David Kelly of BOY TROUBLE who also asked me to contribute several pages, and invited me to share a table with him at APE 2004 in San Francisco.

Realizing I could scarcely face my public (ha ha!) without having created anything new since 1999, I returned to the caffeine and produced 96 new pages for **DON'T BE A CROTTE!** which appeared in spring 2004. I continued my frenetic pace and now have put up a page a day at Keenspace since April 9, 2004. I look forward to continuing to be a presence in the LGBT comics scene.

Andrew "Aethan" French

www.rabco.org/circles, bloopwatch.org, www.livejounal.com/users/aethan

Andy French's published writing career coincides with his decision to come out. Coincidence? Actually, it's because his first professionally published work was in an anthology of gay erotica, and he wanted to tell his parents that he had been published. That story, "Full Moon Fever", can be found in the anthology **WIRED HARD** from Circlet Press. After this came a number of "anthropomorphic animal" stories, on the internet, via the website he shares with his actually legally married husband (thank you Massachusetts), Steve Domanski.

Andy is the co-creator and scripter of **CIRCLES,** a gay, anthropomorphic animal, slice-of-life comic, with husband Steve (layouts), and good buddy Scott Fabianek (pencils & inks.). This series is ongoing, and Andy is very pleased with the reception it's receiving. It is his first work in comics.

K. Sandra Fuhr

www.friendlyhostility.com, www.5ideways.com

Sandra is first and foremost a microbiology/chemistry nerd. The rest of the time, she's drawing, writing, and playing with her ferrets and twenty five thousand billion bettas.

By twenty five thousand billion she means nine. She is very female, born female, happy being female, and has no desire to change this. She has been in a stable relationship for a couple of years, and wishes her partner would clean more often. Seriously, A, that desk is sentient. Sandra follows politics closely, and thus is a very angry person.

Andersen Gabrych

www.dccomics.com

Before writing a fill-in issue of **BATGIRL** and landing the ongoing writing gig on DC Comics' longest-running title, **DETECTIVE COMICS**, Andersen appeared in several feature films, including *Edge of Seventeen*, *The Look*, and *Boys Life 4: Four Play*. He is determined to one day write a series starring the character Vixen.

Steven Gellman (see page 73)

www.hiddenpoet.com

Steven Gellman lives in Germantown, MD with a variety of critters and makes his living as a singer/song-writer.

A huge comic book fan from a young age, Steven is very excited to have just released his brand new comic, **THE ENCHANTERS**, a fantasy/adventure/superhero comic featuring an all gay & lesbian cast of characters.

Steven now divides his time (in between walking his four dogs, of course) between performing and drawing. He is hard at work finishing issue #2 of **THE ENCHANTERS** and working on his fifth CD, entitled *Peaceful World*.

Jade Gordon

jadaze.keenspace.com

I'm a 30 year old, Polyamorous, Pansexual, Divorced (with one current Life Partner), Artist.

LEAN ON ME is my webcomic. It is about an unpopular young woman who meets a suspected cross-dresser at school and falls in love. **LEAN ON ME** has been published on the web since early 2001.

This first chapter involves Yun and J.J. meeting, falling in love, and trying to attend school together as a couple, despite the threats of violence around them. After meeting Yuki and Elizabeth, the four start their own social clique, and conspire to attend the prom as each other's dates.

Diana Green
proggirl@mn.rr.com

Diana Green is a 51-year-old post-op transsexual and has a number of firsts to her credit. She is the first transsexual woman (possibly the first transsexual at all) to earn a BFA in Comic Book Illustration. She created the first dramatic/ humorous transsexual funny animal comic strip for the gay press, **TRANNY TOWERS**, which ran for about a year and a half in Minneapolis' bimonthly *Lavender* magazine; she is the first transsexual woman to self-publish a comic book, **INK TANTRUMS** 1.

She also interned briefly with Reed Waller. Her splotches and unevenly cut zipatone may be seen in **OMAHA, THE CAT DANCER** 13 and 14, and the opening story in **THE COLLECTED OMAHA Vol. 4**.

During her MCAD education, she studied under Peter Gross, Gordon Purcell, Dan Jurgens, Zander Cannon, and Gene Ha! At the request of Gene Ha!, she also served as the model for the superheroine mom Irma Geddon in the DC/ABC series **TOP TEN**.

She is hard at work on a graphic novel version of one of the **TRANNY TOWERS** stories. The new title is **TRANSSCENDING**.

Clayton Kinnelon Greiman
www.gayshakespeare.com

I'm a writer residing in Charlottesville, Virginia. It's always been a dream of mine to write comic books for a living, so I scripted **THE SUIT**, a graphic novel in four chapters.

The awesome news is that I have found a penciller/inker in Mark Brill. He just knocks it out of the ballpark as far as I'm concerned. He states that he should have the art for Chapter One done by the end of November 2005.

Hopefully, in 2006, THE SUIT will be in the hands of many of you who are reading this profile. What a dream come true that will be!

Terrance Griep
www.terrancegriep.com, www.thespiderbaby.com

Best known for his critically acclaimed and oft-reprinted work on DC Comics' **SCOOBY-DOO**, Terrance Griep has left his distinct mark on such icons SUPERMAN, BATMAN, and GREEN LANTERN for that same company, as well. He also contributes to numerous titles for Image Comics. Further, Terrance has scribed his own super-hero creations, **THE SKULKER** and **JOHNNY COSMIC**, both of whom have enjoyed success at various publishers. Current and recent projects include **WITCHGIRLS, INC.**, and **TALES OF THE ARCANE** from Heroic Publishing, as well as **JUDO GIRL**, **VICTORIA'S SECRET SERVICE** and others from BlueWater Productions. A member of the Prism Comics' Advisory Board, he is a writer of that organization's frequently-hit **Queer Eye on Comics** web feature.

For General Mills, Terrance has written several comic strips which featured BuzzBee, the Honey Nut Cheerios mascot. That work was ingested by tens of millions of bleary-eyed readers, appearing in places as varied as cereal boxes and theme park place mats. Terrance also regularly and recklessly ventures into the realm of writing words without pictures. He's worked as a reporter, reviewer, and columnist for a myriad of newspapers and magazines, most notably *OUT*, *The Advocate*, and *Star Trek Monthly*.

Justin Hall [see pages 42, 76]

www.allthumbspress.com

Justin Hall floated to shore on a half-shell and immediately fell in love with comics and chocolate.

He won a 2001 Xeric grant for his first comic **A SACRED TEXT**, a fantastical retelling of the story of the Dead Sea Scrolls. After that he began self-publishing his **TRUE TRAVEL TALES** series, which is a collection of autobiographical and biographical stories from the road, featuring everything from anonymous sex in Egyptian temples to blood sacrifices in Bolivia to smuggling cocaine from Peru. The third **TRUE TRAVEL TALES**, subtitled "**La Rubia Loca**," will be featured in the *Houghton Miflin Best of American Graphic Narratives.*

Hall also has work in various other anthologies, such as the SPX books, *Kitchen Sink Magazine*, **TRUE PORN**, JUICY MOTHER, and more. His character **GLAMAZONIA: THE UNCANNY SUPER TRANNY** has been hard at work making the internet more fabulous, and will be appearing soon in printed form. Hall is also producing an erotic comic **HARD TO SWALLOW** with David Davenport, which will be available early in 2006.

Hall has exhibited his fine art and comics work in New York and San Francisco, including a Small Press Spotlight show at the San Francisco Cartoon Art Museum, where he will be curating a queer cartoonists show in 2006. He is also a comic book convention panel whore, but has finally settled down with moderating the annual Queer Cartoonists Panel at the Alternative Press Expo (APE).

He still loves chocolate and comics, though the ever-growing piles of the latter are taking over the living room and kitchen and making his boyfriend nervous.

Allan Heinberg

Allan Heinberg is an American writer, who currently writes **YOUNG AVENGERS** for Marvel Comics, and has been a writer and producer on *Party of Five*, *Sex and the City*, and *Gilmore Girls*, as well as Co-Executive Producer on the Fox network's series, *The O.C.*

Many cite Heinberg's penchant for American comic books as the reasoning behind constant references to the industry in *The O.C.* Fans consider the show as a great assistance in giving comic books a positive image, as one of the main protagonists, Seth Cohen, has an obsession with comic books. Heinberg also named a supporting character after comic writer Brian Michael Bendis, and has referenced the writer to be Seth's favorite within the show. Heinberg is commonly credited as co-creating the show with Josh Schwartz. Heinberg helped create Orange County's rich cast of immensely popular characters, as well as enriching the overall narrative of the show.

Heinberg states that **YOUNG AVENGERS** will be his only ongoing monthly book, focusing his energies instead on self-contained short arcs or mini-series. The series is widely acclaimed by critics and fans alike. It features the first gay teen superhero couple in a mainstream comic. His stories of coming out and dealing with societal pressures finally explore the long hinted at parallels between being in the closet and the double identities of superheroes.

Victor E. Hodge

blackgayboy.virtualave.net

Victor E. Hodge is a mystery & horror writer, graphic artist and illustrator who lives in Washington, D.C. His multiple passions include collecting DC Direct action figures, **Brenda Starr Reporter** comic strips and customizing black **Barbies**.

BLACK GAY BOY FANTASY, about black gay life in Washington, D.C., began as a one shot strip for the 1996 **Black Lesbian and Gay Pride Guide**. The first issue, an 8-page mini comic, was sold exclusively at Boston's **Outwrite '98**. Those characters also starred in the **LITTLE DRAMAS** comic strip which was featured on the Women In the Life website. His amateur detective, **Rene C. Clayton** is in a short story called "Justifiable Disappearance" under the Spring 1999 edition of Blithe House Quarterly website. His "too short-lived" strip, **FEDERAL BARBEE** appeared in the Department of Interior's **GLOBE** newsletter. This parody was about "America's favorite teen model" going in search of a Federal Government job after the leaving "The Big M!"

Hokane

www.hokane.tk, www.noteesperaba.tk

My name is Carlos Casado, but my penname is Hokane. I was born on October 16, 1978 (Libra) in Mérida (Badajoz), Extremadura's capital, Spain. When I turned 19 years old, I decided to move to the capital of Spain, Madrid. Here I studied graphic design and cartoon animation.

My first profesional comics work was "Reencuentro" in NAUTILUS comics magazine. Other gay comics works are: COCKTAIL TURBULENTO, QUEER IN THE WEST, BETO NUIT BLEU, and BAJO UNA NOCHE ESTRELLADA.

J. Brett Hopkins

www.studio108design.com/jbhopkins, www.brokenland.et/tsg

J. Brett Hopkins is an illustrator living in NYC. His comic book work so far has included soapy 'n' mopey contributions to the **YOUNG BOTTOMS IN LOVE** series, as well as the new, self-published, currently-ongoing miniseries **TWO SHY GUYS**, written by Richard Ruane. In the past, Brett has also been the co-editor of **YBiL**.

Jeff Jacklin

www.jeffsmusclestudio.com

I am an artist/writer whose work has appeared in **GAY COMICS**, **STRIP AIDS USA**, and **MEATMEN**. As a freelancer living in Minneapolis, I worked for a wide spectrum of clients – producing cartoons for the GLBT newspapers **Equal Time** and **GAZE** and the budding skater/punk rock magazine **Your Flesh**, to creating animatics and storyboards for the Department of Defense and its Armed Forces cable channel. I also worked on animation projects such as the title for Fox TV's **Spider-Man**, and CD ROM versions of **Catdog** and **Peter Rabbit.**

I currently live in the southwestern USA, and write and draw **HEARTS & IRON**, a self-published comic book following the continuing adventures of two iron-pumping dudes in love. Two issues have appeared and #3 is on the way. In a 'zine called **Tales From The Queer Side**, I combined a love of science fiction/fantasy and comics.

Patty Jeres

pjeres@nyc.rr.com

Patty Jeres is currently engaged in a personal evolution of sorts, staying active in comics by working in a volunteer capacity for such non-profit organizations as the CBLDF and Prism. Formerly the Director of Marketing Communications for DC Comics at which she had a successful 14-year career, she was well recognized at conventions for being the darling doyenne of the DC booth. Previously, she edited the work of cult cartoonist Matt Howarth, including **THOSE ANNOYING POST BROS**. and **SAVAGE HENRY**. With any luck, by the time you read this entry, she will be well on her way to the next stage of her life.

Phil Jimenez

philjimeneznyc@aol.com

Born and raised in southern California, and trained at NYC's School of Visual Arts, Phil Jimenez has worked in comics since 1991. He first gained recognition for his work on **TEMPEST**. His later works including pencilling stints on the **INVISIBLES**, **JLA-TITANS**, and **PLANETARY/AUTHORITY**. Phil finished a two year run on DC Comics' **WONDER WOMAN**, worked with Grant Morrison on **NEW X-MEN**, and co-authored *The DC Comics Encyclopedia*. His creator-owned project, **OTHERWORLD**, is currently being published through DC/Vertigo, and he is also the penciller on DC's **INFINITE CRISIS**.

Phil's been nominated for Eisner and GLAAD awards, listed as one of *Entertainment Weekly*'s "101 Gay Movers and Shakers," and featured in *The Advocate* and *OUT.* He also created the art for the first permanent AIDS awareness exhibit in the Chicago Museum of Science and Industry and had the good fortune to be Peter Parker's hands, working in a scene as a hand double for Toby Maguire, in *Spider-Man*.

Eric Johnson

www.radioactivepanda.com

I've been writing and drawing the webcomic **RADIOACTIVE PANDA**, for just over two years now. My roomate/web designer and I are just now putting together the first print version of the strip, to be released in early July.

The strip recently underwent a brief hiatus to improve the look, and it seems to have worked. With a little luck I'll eventually be able to pursue this full time.

I've lived in Chicago my whole life and am quite happily attached to a wonderful guy.

David Kelly

www.davidkellystudio.com

I am the creator of **STEVEN'S COMICS**, a comic strip which ran in alternative & gay weeklies such as the *Philadelphia Weekly* and the *Washington Blade* in the mid-1990s. I self-published a collection of strips, **STEVEN'S COMICS: WE ARE FAMILY**, with a grant from the fabulous Xeric Foundation. I also co-edit the comic anthology **BOY TROUBLE**, with co-editor and founder, Robert Kirby.

I am currently working on a follow-up series to **STEVEN'S COMICS** and recently published the fifth issue of the comic anthology **BOY TROUBLE**, "Gay Boy Comics with a New Attitude."

I live in Seattle.

Chip Kidd

Chip Kidd is a graphic designer and writer in New York City. His book jacket designs for Alfred A. Knopf (where he has worked for over fourteen years) have helped spawn a revolution in the art of American book packaging. His work has been featured in *Vanity Fair, Print* (cover story), *Entertainment Weekly, The New Republic, TIME, The New York Times, Graphis, NEW YORK* and *I.D.* magazines. The latter chose him as part of its first **I.D.** 40 group of the nation's top designers and has awarded him "Best of Category, Packaging" twice. In 1997 he received the International Center of Photography's award for Use of Photography in Graphic Design, and he is a regular contributor of visual commentary to the Op-ed page of the *New York Times.* He has been the design consultant for the *Paris Review* since 1995, and in 1998 he was made a member of the Alliance Graphique Internationalle.

Chip Kidd has also written about graphic design and popular culture for **Vogue**, **The New York Times**, **The New York Observer, Entertainment Weekly**, **Details**, **Arena**, **2WICE**, **The New York Post**, **I.D.** and **Print**. His first book as author and designer, **Batman Collected** (1996), was given the Design Distinction award from **ID** magazine, and has just been issued in paperback by Watson-Guptill with an additional 16 pages of new material. His second book, **Batman Animated** (1998) garnered two of the comic book industry's Eisner Awards. Mr. Kidd also designed the acclaimed trilogy of **Superman: The Complete History, Batman: The Complete History** and **Wonder Woman: The Complete History** for Chronicle Books.

Chip Kidd's first novel, **The Cheese Monkeys**, was published by Scribner.

Robert Kirby

www.curb-side.com, www.cleispress.com/Pages/cursideboys.html

Robert Kirby is a Detroit native now living in Minneapolis. His comic strip **CURBSIDE** runs in newspapers across North America.

The first book collection was published by Hobnob Press in 1998 with the aid of a grant from the Xeric Foundation.

The second collection, titled **CURBSIDE BOYS**, was published in October 2002 by Cleis Press, and there is a Spanish edition coming in Fall 2005 from Ediciones La Cupula in Barcelona.

Robert is the founder of the gay boy comics anthology **BOY TROUBLE**, which he co-edits with fellow cartoonist, the lovely and multi-talented David Kelly. The fifth issue, an 80-page trade paperback, was released in 2004. Coming soon, in the Fall of 2006, Green Candy Press of San Francisco will be publishing a book collection reprinting highlights from the first four issues, alongside brand new work by past, present and new contributors.

Randall Kirby

www.bopcomics.com

I have sporadically published my first comic book, **BOP! COMICS**, an all ages superhero comedy. I have a few ready to print, and I'm working on future issues. I dabble in minicomics, and small press pin-up books. I have recently been made associate editor on **YOUNG BOTTOMS IN LOVE** at www.popimage.com, so if you're interested in having a story included, let me know.

Right now I'm working with an AMAZING artist named Brian Douglas Ahern. If you ever get the chance, hire him to draw something for you. I mean it. We're working on a number of projects; some are gay specific, some aren't. (Although they all seem to have an inordinate amount of cute boy characters… hmmm.)

Oh, and I should probably mention that I won the Wizard magazine Halloween costume contest a couple of times. You can also see me modelling as Jeff Byrd in the photos section at www.exhibitapress.com.

Andrew Klaus

www.burntlatexproductions.com

An obsessive-compulsive writer since childhood, Klaus has developed the theological thriller **GODLESS** with illustrator Taylor Vineyard, and the pair will team up again for the post-modern cynicism of **GIRINDA**. Klaus has written for magazines and zines alike on feminist and sexual/gender politics, music, pop culture, art and film.

As if not busy enough with comics and his ever-increasing workload as composer/musician as SOUHADO and guitarist for artpunks SITKA, Klaus is currently at work on a collection of autobiographical essays, **Digging To China** and a painting exhibition entitled **L'Enfants Gris.**

Klaus lives in Portland, Oregon, with his dashingly handsome partner, illustrator and animator Taylor Vineyard.

Steve Korte

www.dccomics.com

Steve Korte is the group editor of the DC Comics Licensed Publishing department. Steve joined DC in 1993, and since then he has edited a wide range of books featuring the DC Comics super heroes, including coffee-table books, novels, and children's books.

Books he has edited include **DC Comics: A Celebration of the World's Favorite Heroes**, **Batman: The Ultimate Evil** by Andrew Vacchs, **Jack Cole and Plastic Man: Forms Stretched to Their Limits** by Art Spiegelman and Chip Kidd (Harvey award winner), **Wonder Woman: The Complete History** (Eisner award winner), and **It's Superman!** by Tom De Haven.

Two of the gayest books he has edited are **TRUER THAN TRUE ROMANCE**, a collection of old romance comics stories with the original art and all-new text by Jeanne Martinet (check out the story "Loving Gay Men!") and **Catwoman: The Life and Times of a Feline Fatale** by Suzan Colon.

Jeff Krell

ignite-ent.com

Jeff Krell created the groundbreaking comic strip **JAYSON**, which debuted in the **Philadelphia Gay News** in 1983. By 1985 **Jayson** had achieved national prominence in **GAY COMIX**, where the strip was named Most Popular Feature. **Jayson** then became a staple in Leyland Publications' **MEATMEN** series of gay male comics anthologies, gracing nearly twenty volumes. In 1990 **JAYSON** debuted in national syndication.

Krell also translated and published English versions of two works by famed German gay cartoonist Ralf König. **MAYBE... MAYBE NOT** and **MAYBE...MAYBE NOT AGAIN!** were the basis for one of Germany's highest grossing comedy movies.

Krell collaborated with singer/songwriters Ron Romanovsky and Paul Phillips to produce an off-Broadway **Jayson** musical at The 45th Street Theatre, which **The New York Times** praised for its "tart, keenly observed humor." The show ran for 10 weeks in the summer of 1998.

Krell's first collection of **Jayson** cartoons, **JAYSON: A NEW COLLECTION** (1997), contained all of the stories that inspired the musical. In 2005 Krell published two new retrospectives, **JAYSON: BEST OF THE 80S** and **JAYSON: BEST OF THE 90S**. He is currently writing new stories for a proposed quarterly **JAYSON** comic book.

Henry Kujawa

www.webspawner.com/users/zodiaccomics/, www.popimage.com/content/ybil401.html

Henry R. Kujawa has been a comic-book fan since 1963 when his parents first bought him a copy of **BLACK FURY** while riding the Chesapeake Bay Ferry Boat.

He began creating his own comics shortly after and first discovered superheroes in January 1966 thanks to the Adam West **Batman** TV show.

STORMBOY #1: STEAL YOUR HEART AWAY is currently available in 6 countries plus the Internet, in part thanks to Bookazine (supplying stores in Germany, The Netherlands, London & Switzerland) and Alamo Square Distributors (mainly the west coast). Henry is currently hard at work on **STORMBOY** #2, which will be a complex espionage-mystery. The new book will also include a 12-page back-up story starring JAY, the hero's rock-singer boyfriend, and other features!

Henry is also working with comics legend Nick Cuti on 2 projects: a new **Moonie (MOONCHILD THE STARBABE)** comic, and *Grub*, a sci-fi movie!

Visit the Zodiac Comics website for previews of the upcoming **STORMBOY** #2 and read Henry's first published comic, **GALACTON 2230**-- free! Also, visit the PopImage.com and read "Dino Rescue", a brand new spin-off story, as well as "I Don't Want To Own You", a 5-page excerpt with Stormboy & Jay!

Jack Lawrence

www.jackademus.com, www.britdoodz.com

I studied Art and Design at Canterbury Technical College and at Canterbury KIAD. I've worked as an animator and freelance illustrator, but my dream was always to work in comics. In May 2003, I made the transition from dreamer to professional when APComics published my creator-owned title, **DARKHAM VALE**. A hopeless control freak, I wrote, pencilled, inked, coloured and lettered **DARKHAM VALE**.

Unfortunately, I hadn't realised that I was signing away the rights to **DARKHAM VALE** in its entirety, not just series by series as I believed. As soon as I joined APC, **DARKHAM VALE** ceased to be creator-owned, so I basically slaved at that comic for virtually nothing.

But, y'know, ya live an' learn, don't ya? I love this industry, and I won't let this nasty experience put me off. Mike Bullock and I are enjoying success with our creator-owned project, **LIONS, TIGERS AND BEARS**, which is published by Image.

I'm also working on a few projects with Kevin Grevioux of **UNDERWORLD** fame, as well as writing a couple of series of my own, to be published in the coming years.

I also run the Britdoodz website and business with my partner, Theo Bain.

Erin Lindsey

venusenvy.keenspace.com

Erin Lindsey is a creative and often excitable artist and writer making her home in the Seattle area. Having a lifetime interest in storytelling in general and illustrated mediums in particular, Erin has been a published cartoonist since her days in middle school, as well as having written articles for a handful of small journals and gaming magazines.

Her current claim to fame is the online comic and independent comic book **VENUS ENVY**, the story of a neurotic young woman trying her best to survive despite a few amusingly cruel mistakes of nature. **VENUS ENVY** has been running continuously for over two years and continues to draw an excess of 150,000 visitors per day.

Erin is a self-proclaimed sporty geek, enjoying comic books, anime, roleplaying games, baking, roller-blading, rock climbing, and keeping a tight leash on her evil mutant spider clone, Erin 2.0.

Kasey Loman

www.hippieandbulldyke.com/

I'm the author and creator of **HIPPIE AND BULLDYKE**, a webcomic available at hippieandbulldyke.com.

Inspired by real people, **HIPPIE AND BULLDYKE** relates the adventures of two lesbians as they tackle harrowing political and cultural issues in a satirical fashion. Meet such characters as Earth Cookie, a crunchy save-the-world personality, and Bigotron, an evil Republican robot (a.k.a. George W. Bush).

New comics are posted each Tuesday, and readers have the opportunity to become a character in **Hippie and Bulldyke** by sending a photo and brief essay.

Michael Lovitz

www.cblh.com

A long-time comic book fan, Michael spent his youth (and all of his years since) immersed in this most compelling art form. Soon, his fancy turned to a broader range of popular culture, from science fiction to animation. An avid Warner fan and DisneyWorld aficionado, Michael, an attorney specializing in trademark and copyright law, has managed to merge his career with his hobby, representing creators and companies in the comic book industry. Although he still dreams of someday being a comic book writer, Michael has written extensively about the comic book industry, and is the author of a legal guide for comic book creators—*The Trademark & Copyright Book* (May 2001, Sirius Entertainment). Michael has also completed the script for an expanded edition, which will include sections on licensing and infringements.

Steve MacIsaac (see page 52)

www.stevemacisaac.com

I'm a Canadian currently living in Southern California after almost four years in Japan. My work's been in a number of zines and anthologies, including HOLY TITCLAMPS, WHAT'S WRONG?, **TRUE PORN**, and **BOY TROUBLE**.

I am also the artist on **STICKY**, a series of erotic short stories done in collaboration with writer Dale Lazarov. Three issues were published by Eros Comics and which will be collected in a hardcover in April 2006. April will also be the month I start a new comic book series called **SHIRTLIFTER**, supported in part by the fine folks at Prism Comics and their **Queer Press Grant**.

You can see some preview images from **STICKY** and my other work on my website.

Leo Magna

www.LionDogWorks.com

Well there is not a lot to say about me. I live in the sunny state of California, in the quiet (and not so quiet) city of Santa Monica. Currently a college student, and that is what steals my time from my drawing desk.

Started drawing some time ago, and finally decided to put something up there for myself (LionDogWorks. com being that something). I've been a fur since 2001? 2002? don't remember.

Ermm... well nothing else comes to mind, but I'll post up anything else that comes to mind.

If any other questions come up, I'll answer them.

Timothy Markin

adacat100@aol.com

Creator of **BREAKNECK BLVD**, artist/writer Timothy Markin was born in 1968 and raised in a suburb of Toledo, Ohio. Interested in comics of all types at an early age, he began pursuing a career in cartooning in his teens.

Before moving to Kansas City, Markin had a stint in the USMC stationed near Washington DC, where the ideas for **BREAKNECK BLVD** first started to germinate.. The book told the story of everyman Urban Angst, his exotic dancer friend Scarlett Dee, and openly gay writer Pall Blighter. Local publisher MotioN Comics put **BREAKNECK BLVD** in print where it was then noticed by San Jose alternative publisher Slave Labor Graphics. Six issues of the book were published by SLG in 1995 and 1996.

Markin also did two stories for SLG's adaptation of John Marr's **MURDER CAN BE FUN** zine, one of which was a retelling of the true-life incident that inspired the film *Dog Day Afternoon*.

Currently, Markin is working on a new series, looking for a new publisher and living with his wife, two dogs and four cats in Erie, Pennsylvania.

Laz Marquez

www.lazmarquez.com

Born and raised in the New York City area, Laz Marquez began his artistic endeavors very early in life. He obtained his initial training in Fine Arts (specifically the art of oil and sumi painting) and progressed onward to explore the world of digital artwork and illustration. Most of his work has been described specifically as haunting, having an element of sadness but remaining true to the beauty of reality.

Now, Laz Marquez is a working graphic designer, specializing in print design and digital illustration. He also uses most of his un-used time to illustrate various comic book projects in which he has taken the initiative to create.

Laz Marquez has created works for many off-Broadway productions (including *Oz*, *The Ultimate Drag Off!* and *Media Killed the Video Star*), as well as a few movie studio projects for conceptual and movie poster artwork. He also offers freelance design services at his website, www.lazmarquez.com.

Michael Marriner

www.boy-sluts.com, yaoi.y-gallery.net/user/scooterx/

I"ve been drawing comics for about seven years. My interest in comics is mostly through Japanese manga and anime, especially yaoi and shoujo ("girls") genres.

My first comic was published in the 2nd Yaoi-Con anthology SHONEN HUMP. My second published work is the first of my BOY SLUTS stories, and can be found in SHONEN volume 1. The Boy Sluts are a parody of the Boy Scouts—they exist in a sex-positive world where young men's affections for one another are fostered.

I also dabble in other gay erotica - furry, S/M, and some fanart.

Greg McElhatton

www.iComics.com, www.ninthart.com/tocome, www.Spxpo.com, www.marathongreg.com

Greg McElhatton has written reviews about comics of all shapes and sizes for iComics.com since 1999 after an ill-timed, "Sure, I'd love to write a review or two" snowballed horribly out of control.

In addition, Greg has been involved with running the Small Press Expo (SPX) since 1998, including taking the role of Executive Director for SPX 2002 and 2003.

Last but certainly not least, he currently writes THINGS TO COME for Ninth Art, was an Eisner Awards judge in 2002, has co-edited two of the SPX anthologies, and contributed an essay to the 2005 edition of St. Martin's Press's *Year's Best Graphic Novels, Comics & Manga.*

In his spare time he runs marathons.

Craig McKenney

www.headshakepress.com

Xeric-award winner Craig McKenney writes and/or publishes the fine line of books from Headless Shakespeare Press.

His most recent 3-issue miniseries is **THE BRONTES: INFERNAL ANGRIA**. Illustrated by Rick Geary, the 2nd issue should be out in early 2006.

His next project, **KIRBY**, is well under way. Illustrated by Mosquito, it should be out in early 2007.

Chaos McKenzie

www.goldenbulletstudio.com

Chaos McKenzie. Writer. Producer. Provoker. 26. Creative Crackpot. @ 22 was meddling with media constructed reality with Much Music, ChumCity, Bravo!, and Alliance Atlantis. @ 23 sold first works to Humanoids

Publishing for their **METAL HURLANT** anthology and hopes to do more. Controversial works have appeared in *Hive Magazine*, *Katalogue Arts Zine* (www.katalogue.ca), *Neksis Magazine*, *Xtra! Magazine*, *The Naked News*, and comic reviews on Ain't It Cool News. Has some plans. Going to stir things up.

Currently working on a series of self contained comic stories meant to celebrate the diversity of genre, theme and character, in slice of life, magical blends of art and word found within comic books of any and all kinds. Upcoming projects include **ROAD TRIP 666** with Jason Reeves, **PSYCHIC FRIENDS NETWORK** with Miles Collins, and **SHUURAAH!**, with character designs by Scott Hepburn.

Chuck McKinney

www.fromthecellarnyc.com

Hi there. Chuck McKinney here, creator of the gay comic strip, **FROM THE CELLAR**.

A little over a year ago, I was bartending in a restaurant in downtown Manhattan. The owners lost their lease and had to close, but at the same time, they were about to open their first ever **gay bar**. That's where I ended up. When I moved to New York over 10 years ago (to be an actor), I never would have guessed I would end up bartending in a gay bar. To my surprise, I enjoy it. The DJs are great, the go-go boys are plentiful, and my coworkers are lots of fun. It's more like being out and having a good time, except I have the protection of having the bar between me and everyone else, and I leave with money in my pocket.

It wasn't long before I realized I should be documenting this chapter of my life in some way. **FROM THE CELLAR** is just that: gay nightlife from behind the scenes and behind the bar.

There's a lot more to come. I find a new artist for each episode; that's the slow part. So if there are any artists out there who are comfortable with the eight-panel grid and can draw cute guys, please contact me.

Kyle Minor

www.cake-club.com/kyle

Kyle is a long-time comics fan and is past Central Mailer and President of NORTHSTAR-APA. He lives and works in San Francisco, and only sings karaoke once in a while. He helped see *Out in Comics* and *Prism Comics: Your LGBT Guide to Comics* get made from 2000 through 2003. Currently he is one of the writers of Prism Comics' popular **Queer Eye on Comics** weekly review series.

Rumors that romantically connect him to only the really really nice gay porn stars are purely speculative.

Bevis Musson

www.factorfictionpress.co.uk/girly, www.Gayleague.com/online/qod/qodintro.php

Bevis Musson is an example of how if you want to make comics then you shouldn't let anything get in your way. Although most of his work has been printed as regular comics the internet has enabled him to get his work seen by more people than would be possible if he were just to follow the self publishing route.

Bevis is the creator, writer, artist and letterer of **THE QUEEN OF DIAMONDS**, a slightly unconventional superhero comic about an unashamedly gay hero defending his city and trying to have some kind of life at the same time. **THE QUEEN OF DIAMONDS** can be found at The Gay League and is updated as and when Bevis gets time to do it.

Bevis is also the artist on **ODDCASES**, working with writer Alistair Pulling. **ODDCASES** follows the adventures of two middle-aged ladies in comfortable shoes as they investigate and deal with paranormal matters. The series has been described as *Two Fat Ladies* meets *The X-Files* (but without Mulder's scary lack of chin). The early **ODDCASES** adventures can be found at Opi8 and later adventures have been published as part of the **GIRLY COMIC** anthologies.

Bevis has also done various work for JUST 1 PAGE, SMUT PEDDLER and CYBEROSIA.

Bevis lives in Manchester, UK, with his partner and their insane cat Max.

Allan Neuwirth
www.chelseaboys.com, www.animatorsink.com/fetured/allan.html

Allan Neuwirth is a native New Yorker who writes, creates, develops, produces, directs, and designs animated TV series, screenplays, books, a syndicated comic strip, comic books & graphic novels, games, music videos, and award-winning animated TV commercials.

In 1998, with illustrator/writer Glen Hanson (designer of MTV's *Spy Groove*), Allan co-created the popular comic strip **CHELSEA BOYS**, currently syndicated in dozens of publications and websites all across the U.S., as well as Canada and the UK. In 2003, Alyson Books published the first bound **CHELSEA BOYS** collection. Allan & Glen recently signed a deal with MTV's new all gay network LOGO to develop the strip as an animated TV series. Allan has also worked on several cartoons and authored books on animation and television comedy.

Allan has dabbled in many other creative pursuits: penned comic book scripts for D.C. Comics (the **FLINTSTONES** & **JETSONS** series, and the REALWORLDS: WONDER WOMAN graphic novel), directed off-Broadway plays (*The Butter & Egg Man*, *City Lights*), designed theatrical posters & Playbill covers for the legendary Phoenix Theater, written standup comedy material for Regis Philbin and others, performed voice-overs for cartoons and animated commercials, and art directed five seasons of Joan Lunden's ACE Award-winning TV series *Mother's Day* for Lifetime Television.

His children's books include *Frankenstein Lives!, Dracula Is Coming!, Barbie: Party Time!, Barbie: Super Water Skier, Scottie Pippen: Power Shooter!*, and *Patrick Ewing: High Flyer.*

Currently he's directing & producing a live action musical comedy TV special called *Abbalicious*, featuring NYC's most famous and talented drag performers singing ABBA's greatest hits.

Terri Noble
www.martharick.com

Terri Noble, a once-young tranny trying to find a life, has been drawing for as long as she can remember.

Inspired by her lesbian cousin, Terri began her webcomic MARTHA AND RICK AMONG OTHERS, the mildly diverting tale of a dyke and a straight guy sharing living quarters. Terri insists it is **not** a ripoff of *Will and Grace*.

The comic has developed a small following, and even that is diminishing due to Terri's decreasing updates. However, she believes there is something of worth in her creation and persists in plugging away.

François Peneaud

gaycomicslist.free.fr, frpeneaud.free.fr

I'm a French comics reader who mainly writes about LGBT-themed comics, but reads all kinds of comics (including bandes dessinées in my native language and mangas in English & French).

With my Gay Comics List site, I intend to provide a large and varied view of those queer comics - that and it gives me a good excuse to be in contact with a lot of creators whose work I enjoy.

Outside of comics critique (which I also do for a French site), I've been very happy to write three stories for the gay online anthology **YOUNG BOTTOMS IN LOVE**, including one upcoming in the current volume, and I'm trying to find publishers for various scripts I've worked on.

As for more personal details, I'll say that I'm in my late 30's and live in the South West of France with my long-suffering partner (he's got his own obsessive hobby, so don't pity him too much).

Joe Phillips

www.joephillips.com, www.imrufan.com

I got into comics when my brother suggested that I should draw comics and I figured I'd give it a shot. I went to all sorts of comic and sci-fi conventions with my portfolio with drawings super heroes and dragons. I soon got work for a small comic company doing a book called **SOUTHERN KNIGHTS**. After that came a run on **SPEED RACERS** comic for 8 issues and then on to **THE VAMPIRE LESTAT** and later **INTERVIEW WITH THE VAMPIRE**. It was only a matter of time before I was at DC Comics and drawing **MISTER MIRACLE** and **JLA**. After that I was hooked and for the next 15 years I did every comic and every comic book company out there. I even had my own book, **THE HERETIC**, from Dark Horse out for a while. I was one of the founding members of Gaijin Studio in Atlanta with Brian Stelfreeze, Karl Story, Adam Hughes, Tony Harris, Jason Pearson, Cully Hamner, Dave Johnson and Christien Walsh. For a time we were this brash new breed of comic artists that redefined craftsmanship and story telling in our panel layout and painted covers.

I left the studio after 3 years and moved into my home studio. I was drawing everything from **SILVER SURFER** to painted trading cards. It was a great ride but the bottom fell out of the industry with multiple copies and variant covers and the spectators left and little comic shops went bankrupt and artists lost clients.

As time past I was growing weary of the same thing week after week. I finally left comics after an artistic breakdown where I couldn't draw for nearly a month. I was done with traditional comics and needed a break. Of course, as fate would have it didn't take long before I stumbled on to **XY** magazine and start doing a gay strip in their mag. I later started a gay product company along with my friends Tim Wayne and Nick Reedy. We named it **Xodus USA**–after all, it had a cool X in it and it was one of the few words we could all agree on. I created the "Joe Boy Dress Me" magnets and drew all the designs for the website and t-shirts.

During that period I was approached by 10% productions and launched my "Boys Will be Boys" calendar series and my cards. A friend of mine from back in the comic days named Chad had secured joephillips.com for me as a gift and I opened the Joe Boys to the web with a site created for me by Tim and later updated by my brother Lex.

One of Chad's other jobs was as webmaster to a few adult websites. They wanted an adult cartoon and Chad suggested me, and before you know it me and my now ex-boyfriend were animating porn on Kara's Adult Playground with a **Star Trek** spoof named "Cumquest," soon followed on Absolutely Male with **"House of Morecock."** After a year of this I formed a new company, Adult Visual Animation, with my brother and friend Ron Mcfee and packaged up the web-episodes along with a few new images and released **Morecock** on DVD with 10% and Green Wood Cooper.

Michael Phillips

groups.yahoo.com/group/Northstar-ATDNSIN

Mike Phillips has been an avid comic book fan since 1960 when he noticed the skin-tight costumes on The Flash and Green Lantern and how they always seemed to ditch their girlfriends to run off together. He also noticed that Batman and Robin seemed to be spending too much time together, if you know what I mean. In 1989 he became involved in amateur press associations and currently acts as coordinator for "The APA That Dares Now Speak Its Name", founded by Andy Mangels, and also "Northstar" APA, founded by Jericho Wilson.

Mike has created a universe of LGBT characters of his own with the intention of eventual self-publishing but for now has turned his attention to filmmaking where he intends to make films about the LGBT experience.

Currently he is working on a documentary film about LGBT comic book fandom tentatively called SECRET IDENTITIES which will include fans, creators, character images, animation, and anyone supportive of LGBT characters and their creators. Please contact him if you would like to be included in interviews for this project.

Brad Rader

www.flamingartist.com

Brad Rader has wanted to draw comics since he was twelve, but most of his career has been spent doing storyboards on animated television series such as **Batman: The Animated Series**, **Gargoyles**, and **Men In Black**. Brad was also Animation Director of **Roswell Conspiracies** and **Space Monkeys** on UPN. His work with the team that produces **Spawn** for HBO won him a primetime Emmy Award in 1999, for Outstanding Animated Program (programming of more than one hour).

He finally got the opportunity to do comics back in the early 1990's working on DC's **THE BATMAN ADVENTURES** (issues 4–6), and on **THE MARK** for Dark Horse. More recently he pencilled seven issues of **CATWOMAN** for DC, as well as a fill-in issue of **GOTHAM ADVENTURES**, **FUSE** #3 for Image, and **FUSED: CANNED HEAT** for Dark Horse.

From there he moved back to storyboarding, on **Stripperella** (Nickelodeon), **Megas XLR** (Cartoon Network), and **Legends of the Dragon** (Tom T Animation).

Now he is embarking on the adventure of self-publishing. His first venture is **TRUE ADULT FANTASY** volumes 1 and 2, which are compilations of 20+ years of his erotic sketchbooks and also contain four episodes of a gay soap opera about hard-driving truckdrivers, transsexuality 'n' stuff. They're available at his website. Recently he worked on the Bush-bashing collaboration **TEX**—check out the animated trailer for the book at JoshuaDysart.com/tex.html.

Jacki Randall

jackirandall.com, tattooartists.org, bodyartweb.com, bmezine.com, dykesonbikes.org

For Jacki, being an artist and musician is as natural as breathing and her love for women. Her cartoons have been characterized as politically incorrect, anti-woman, and just downright dirty in reflecting her experience, so they're not for just anybody!

In addition to cartooning, Jacki's portfolio consists of erotica, spiritual icons, murals, paintings, illustrations, and tattooing. Aside from numerous publications, her early endeavors appeared in the **Baltimore Gaypaper** which began running her dyketoons in 1981, **GAY COMICS**, and her most recent works which appear in a number of tattoo art magazines. She continues to play guitar and compose, as well as write and paint.

Jacki met her partner Robin while living in Baltimore in September of 1989. Since then they have lived in San Francisco, Albuquerque, and for over a decade in Portland, Oregon. Jacki is a professional tattoo artist in Maryland. You can reach her through her website, jackirandall.com.

Mikhaela Reid
www.mikhaela.net

Mikhaela B. Reid is a 25-year-old political cartoonist for the **Boston Phoenix** and **Bay Windows** (Boston's LGBT newspaper). Her work has also appeared in **Women's eNews**, **Ms.**, **Girlfriends**, **The Minnesota Women's Press**, **Inside Pride** and other assorted fine publications. She is also featured as "cartooning's angry young woman" in the anthology **ATTITUDE 2: THE NEW SUBVERSIVE ALTERNATIVE CARTOONISTS**, edited by Ted Rall. Her weekly cartoons are available in color or black and white for reprint in print and online publications.

Mikhaela was born and raised in Lowell, Massachusetts, where she attended Lowell High School and served as president of the Lowell High School Rainbow Connection Gay/Straight Alliance. More recently, she graduated from Harvard University, where she studied social anthropology and photography and did weekly political cartoons for the **Harvard Crimson.** Currently she works full-time as an information graphics artist designing graphs and charts for a major daily newspaper. She lives in Brooklyn with her cat Riley.

Laila Reimoz
www.yaoipress.com

Laila Reimoz is the Editor of Yaoi Press, a lesbian-owned publisher of original English language yaoi graphic novels. Yaoi Press seeks to produce original yaoi manga of the highest caliber and will publish six books in 2005 alone. Yaoi Press tailor its books specifically for Western audiences, and strives to create titles that appeal to both women and homosexual men. In 2006 Yaoi Press will partner with a major video game company and create at least one yaoi video game.

Yaoi Press is always looking for new talent.

Jennifer Reitz
www.PastelDefender.com, www.UnicornJelly.com, www.Jenniverse.com, www.Transsexual.org

Jennifer Diane Reitz is a former game designer and game illustrator turned online cartoonist. She lives in Washington with her three polyamoric spouses. She creates science fiction comics that promote a positive Queer identity.

Her webcomics include **PASTEL DEFENDER HELIOTROPE**, the fully hand-painted story of a mysteriously animated artificial being and her quest for identity within a strange universe with unique physical laws. **PASTEL DEFENDER HELIOTROPE** examines the nature of what it means to be alive, and the impact of the individual upon society, all against a backdrop of unique and alien cosmological events.

Sara Rojo Pérez (see page 88)
www.sararojo.com

Born in Madrid in 1973.

Former Artistic and Creative Director of Spanish animation studio Sopa de Sobre.

Illustrator of numerous children's books in Spain, the U.S., and elsewhere, including **Fur, Fangs, and Footprints: A Collection of Poems About Animals**, **The Free and the Brave: A Collection of Poems About the United States**, **Cobwebs, Chatters, and Chills: A Collection of Scary Poems**, and **Recess, Rhyme, and Reason: A Collection of Poems About School**.

Comics work include the forthcoming color graphic novel **MIXED BLESSINGS** (Germany: Heinz und Horst Verlag) and the black and white comic series **A COFFIN FOR TWO** (US: NBM Publishing), as well as the short story "The Anniversary" in **JUICY MOTHER 2** (US: Soft Skull), all with scripts by Lawrence Schimel.

Regular illustrator for Spanish magazine **Vanity Gay**.

P. Craig Russell

www.lurid.com, frpeneaud.free.fr/artists/Russell/RussellPresentation.html

A graduate of the University of Cincinnati with a degree in painting, Philip Craig Russell has run the gamut in comics. After establishing a name for himself at Marvel, he went on to become one of the pioneers in opening new vistas for this underestimated field with, among other works, adaptations of operas by Wagner (**Parsifal**) and Mozart (**The Magic Flute**). He has become an "artist's artist" with his fine-lined realistic style.

A winner of a Harvey Award, many Eisner Awards, and the Inkpot Award for Career Achievement, Craig came out to the industry in a 1991 interview in **The Comics Journal** #147, where he referred to himself as "just another left-handed, night-dwelling, gay libertarian cartoonist."

His collected comics work includes **9-11: ARTISTS RESPOND, volume 1; CONAN AND THE JEWELS OF GWAHLUR; ELRIC: STORMBRINGER; two volumes of the FAIRY TALES OF OSCAR WILDE; GOTHAM BY GASLIGHT: A TALE OF THE BATMAN; HELLBOY: WEIRD TALES, volume 2; ISOLATION AND ILLUSION: COLLECTED SHORT STORIES OF P. CRAIG RUSSELL; MURDER MYSTERIES; PAGLIACCI: THE CLOWNS; STAR WARS: CRIMSON EMPIRE, volume 1, THE P. CRAIG RUSSELL LIBRARY OF OPERA ADAPTATIONS; THE RING OF THE NIBELUNG Books 1 and 2, and THE SCARLET LETTER.**

Stephen Sadowski

clubs.yahoo.com/clubs/sadowskiappreciationdivision

Born and raised in British Columbia, Canada, Stephen Sadowski grew up collecting everything comic-related he could. He has been publicly "out" for about 20 years or so, and realized his boyhood dream of working for DC Comics, as penciller for one of DC's biggest successes, **JSA**.

Steve's work includes Malibu Comics' **FIREARM** 13 (10 pages un-credited), **JESTERCROW** 1 from Castle Rain, **Bob Burden's MYSTERY MEN** 1 and 2 from Dark Horse, and for DC, **STARMAN** 56 and **STARMAN 80-PAGE GIANT, SMASH COMICS 1, ALL STAR COMICS 2, JSA SECRET FILES, POWER COMPANY, JLA/JSA SECRET FILES, JSA ALL STARS: DOCTOR MIDNITE,** and **WONDER WOMAN**, as well as **PARADISE X: DEVILS** and **THE AVENGERS from Marvel.**

He has also worked doing storyboards for motion pictures, video games and commercials.

Gregory Sanchez

www.gayleague.com/studio/fanfic/index.php?id=5

Florida-born, California-raised, and currently hailing from Denver, Colorado, Greg is the creator and writer of the GLBT series of super-hero novels, **RAINBOW ARC OF FIRE**.

First begun in the late summer of 1994, and first published in fall of 1996, the series now consists of ten novels, the first eight of which are available in book form, with the remaining two novels currently published online at the Gay League Web site.

RAINBOW ARC OF FIRE merges the real-life experiences of the author and the contemporary locations where those experiences have taken place with these several fictional characters and their extraordinary escapades, to provide tales in which the diverse sexuality of those characters becomes the perspective through which they view the world and the world views them.

Relationships, Colorado's Amendment 2, gays in the military, gay marriage, AIDS, prejudice, and many more issues and concerns of GLBT individuals play out in locales as diverse as The Rocky Mountains; The U.S. Air Force Academy; Denver, Colorado; Yellowstone National Park; the Underworld of the Greek Gods, Hades; Europe; Asia; and, eventually, outer space. These may be super-powered beings, but they are still, and primarily, human beings.

The series has been the author's life's work and absorbing passion. Whether there will be more novels in the series, only time and circumstance will tell.

Lawrence Schimel (see page 28, 88)

www.circlet.com/schimel.html

Lawrence Schimel was born in New York City on 16 October 1971 and is currently living in Madrid, Spain.

He is an award-winning author and anthologist, who has published over 70 books in a wide variety of genres, including fiction, cooking, gender studies, sports, poetry--and of course comics!

Working primarily with the Spanish artist Sara Rojo Pérez, together they've produced numerous children's titles in Spanish such as *Manual práctico para viajar en OVNI* (la osa menor), *Misterio en el Jardín* (Kalandraka), *La aventura de Cecilia y el dragón* (la osa menor), and a recent album celebrating gay families *Amigos y vecinos* (Ediciones La Librería).

Schimel and Rojo have a number of forthcoming comics projects as well, including:

a short black and white story, "The Anniversary," in Jennifer Camper's anthology **JUICY MOTHER 2** (Soft Kkull) and also excerpted in the **2006 Prism Guide (see p.XX)**;

a full-color graphic novel titled **MIXED BLESSINGS**, about a gay WASP and a gay Jew in NYC who decide to get married and how their families react, for German publisher Heinz und Horst verlag; and

a back and white romantic comedy about vampires, **A COFFIN FOR TWO**, with a strong gay subplot, for NBM publishing.

An earlier graphic novel, **VACACIONES EN IBIZA** (**Vacation in Ibiza**), illustrated in color by Catalan comics artist Sebas, is published in Spain by Egales, in the U.S. by NBM Publishing, and in Germany from Heinz und Horst. The American edition was a finalist for the Lambda Literary Award.

Schimel is a contributor to the comics-related anthologies *The Sandman: Book of Dreams* edited by Neil Gaiman (HarperCollins) and *Superheroes* edited by John Varley (Berkeley), and has also translated graphic novels (by Segrelles, etc.) from Spanish into English for NBM Publishing.

Most recently, he's turned his attention to books exploring and reconciling Judaism and homosexuality, with the anthologies *Kosher Meat* (Sherman Asher) exploring sexuality, which was a finalist for both Lambda Literary Award and the ForeWord Book of the Year Award, and *Found Tribe: Jewish Coming Out Stories* (Sherman Asher) dealing with issues of community, which was a double-finalist for the Lambda Literary Award and also a finalist for the ForeWord Book of the Year Award. Both titles were selections of the InsightOut Book Club and Traditions Jewish Book Club.

For two years he served as co-chair of the Publishing Triangle, the organization of lesbians and gay men in the publishing industry, responsible for National Lesbian and Gay Book Month, BookAIDS (a program which delivers over 40,000 books free to PWAs each year), an annual awards series, and numerous other programs and events.

Bob Schreck

www.dccomics.com

Bob Schreck is a Group Editor in the DC Universe editorial department. He began his career in marketing, promotions and administration, working for Creation Conventions, Marvel Comics, and Comico, and rose to the position of Marketing Director at Dark Horse Comics in 1990. At Dark Horse, Bob changed gears and became Senior Group Editor, where he edited such projects as SIN CITY by Frank Miller and **MADMAN** by Michael Allred, and won two consecutive Harvey Awards as editor of the groundbreaking anthology **DARK HORSE PRESENTS**.

Bob left Dark Horse in 1996 to co-found Oni Press with Joe Nozemack. There he developed such projects as **CLERKS: THE COMIC BOOK** and **JAY & SILENT BOB** with screenwriter and director Kevin Smith, as well as the Harvey Award winning anthology **ONI DOUBLE FEATURE** and the critically acclaimed **WHITEOUT** by Greg Rucka and Steve Leiber.

Bob currently edits DC's **All Star** line which includes **BATMAN & ROBIN THE BOY WONDER** by Frank Miller & Jim Lee and **SUPERMAN** by Grant Morrison & Frank Quitely, and Matt Wagner's **BATMAN & THE MONSTER MEN**, among many others.

Richard A. Scott

www.geocities.com/soho/studios/9720/index.html

Richard A. Scott is an artist born and raised in Anchorage, Alaska, and who's currently living in Portland, Oregon.

Richard's previous work includes being a staff artist for *Science Fiction Review*, a non-credited inking assist on the DC Comics/TSR book **AVATAR** #1, and the **COMMITTED COMICS CONVENTION SPECIAL**.

He's worked on several research projects with Andy Mangels, such as *Animation on DVD*, *From Scream to Dawson's Creek: An Unauthorized Take on the Phenomenal Career of Kevin Williamson*, the *Comics Buyers Guide* #1441 DVD cover story, and Robert James Parish's *Gus Van Sant: An Unauthorized Biography*.

Richard is currently seeking paying gigs, and invites you to visit his web page for more info.

Sean-Z

www.sean-z.com

Sean-Z (aka Sean Holman) has been creating art on paper since he was 3 years old.

Eventually, he found his way to the Windy City where he attended the School of the Art Institute of Chicago, honing his artistic skills in the areas of illustration, animation and graphic design.

After working as a freelance graphic designer for nearly 3 years, he decided that he needed a major change of pace, which included the decision to never again live in a city where both snow and extremely cold temperatures were the norm.

After much thought, and at the behest and encouragement of a few close friends and family members, he decided to take a big leap (in more ways than one) and move to Los Angeles and pursue his first love: story-telling with his art. Most of his work falls under the Sci-Fi, Fantasy and Gay Erotic genres, though he is by no means limited to those categories.

He considers himself an "A to Z" Artist—which simply means that he has no limitations as to what he will create, so long as he feels that it is within him to do so.

MYTH is Sean-Z's first published comic book.

Trisha L. Sebastian

www.saucygoosepress.com, www.sequentialtart.com

Trisha L. Sebastian is a writer, editor, occasional karaoke singer and all-around hot muchacha. The former associate editor of *Wizard: Anime Insider*, she's back in the freelance writer's pool where she writes far too much on far too little sleep.

She's also the webmistress for Saucy Goose Press, the director of Guest Relations for Anime Next and co-helmed the 2004 24-Hour MiniComics Challenge with Pam Bliss. She's always got her irons in the fire.

Eric Shanower

www.age-of-bronze.com, www.hungrytigerpress.com, www.ericshanower.com

Most of the major US comic book publishers have published work of mine. Some of that work has won awards and some of it has sunk into the oblivion of time, which may be just as well. While I've been writing and drawing comics, I've also written and illustrated books, drawn magazine and trading card illustrations, and created artwork for a couple television projects.

The comics I'm most proud of are my **OZ** graphic novel series and **AN ACCIDENTAL DEATH** with writer Ed Brubaker, neither of which contain overt queer content (although **OZ** has a big queer following and Charlie in **AN ACCIDENTAL DEATH** certainly should set off your gaydar). I'm also proud of my current comic book series **AGE OF BRONZE** which tells my version of the Trojan War drawn from both the literary and artistic tradition and from the archaeology of the places and cultures involved. **AGE OF BRONZE** certainly has queer content, most visibly in the relationship between Achilles and Patroklus. If you're interested in my other work, there's a list of credits on my web site ericshanower.com.

I live in San Diego with my partner, David Maxine, and our Boston terrier, Road. When I'm not working, I'm often reading, swimming, taking ballet lessons, or just trying to make sure I get out of the house once in a while.

Rhys-Michael Silverlocke

www.bloodandbrimstone.com/corwyn/story.html

Rhys-Michael Silverlocke was born on the cusp of libra and some other horoscopic sign—the name of which momentarily escapes memory. (Thank god that "astrology" is complete and utter rubbish or Mr. Silverlocke might have suffered a bizarre concatenation of celestial eventualities. [Thank astrology that "god" is also complete and utter rubbish.] Astrology and religions are just nice opportunities for people to say pretentious and superficial things like "Oh I would **never** eat sushi with someone who wasn't born in the year of the Rat".)

When not speaking parenthetically, Mr. Silverlocke is probably speaking pedantically, or possibly inaudibly and entirely for his own amusement. In any case, the operative concept is that he rarely stops speaking; when he gets a few hundred thousand words left over that no one in the immediate area desires hearing then he generally sets them down into novel form.

Mr. Silverlocke has written many novels; his short stories, pressed into hardwood, can be used to construct an elegant 18th century provincial armoire. He is a writer, pianist, guitarist, composer and chef… but sadly none of his creations to date have proved truly toyetic and thus are not available with a "value meal" at any local fast-food chain.

Currently, he authors a series for *Instinct* magazine entitled BLOOD & BRIMSTONE which makes less and less sense as the artist cuts each new panel from the script.

Note: The lucky "Jesus loves a Taurus" t-shirts are still available for sale on his website! Supplies are limited so order yours today!

Paul Slattery

es-cb.netinertia.co.uk

I fell in love with Silver Age Marvel, and try to capture those elements of characterisation and continuity in my own work - albeit in a more contemporary context, with a cosmopolitan cast that embraces pretty much every orientation, sexual or otherwise, in what I hope is a frank and realistic fashion.

For me, the characters and storylines come first. While I accept that it is a required aspect of the genre I've chosen to write in, I actually find the whole 'ZAP!', 'POW!' thing more of a chore to write than the quieter moments. That said, I feel the artist is a vital part of the storytelling process, and can probably convey that side of things far better than I can.

I see creating comics as a collaborative process, and am always open to input from others. Yes, I have a certain vision - I've spent decades putting this fictional universe together, giving it a beginning, middle and end - but now that I have come to put the flesh on the bones there is plenty of scope for improvisation, so it is unlikely that I would ever say 'No, we can't do that', or 'No, I don't think that would work'.

The scripts on my site are mostly first drafts, though I have made a few alterations here and there. I'm currently looking for collaborators, and a way to bring this material to print without losing creative control, which seems to be the trickiest part right now, so any advice would be more than welcome.

Jeremy Smith

www.candlelightpress.com, www.designbyjeremy.com

I was born and raised in the heartland, a no-nonsense boy with a silly streak.

I illustrate graphic novels with Candle Light Press, an independent small press growing our own books our own way here in the fertile soil in and around Iowa City, Iowa. We are a "print-on-demand" operation, and our books are available wherever books are sold. I am not a "name" in the industry (yet), but hope one day to do this for a living. In addition to some freelance graphic design work locally, I am the artist on four books by CLP: **NUMBERS: A TALE OF SHADES & ANGELS**, **THE FAIRER SEX: A TALE OF SHADES & ANGELS**, **ZOO FORCE: DEAR ENIKO** and **ZOO FORCE: BEAN & NOTHINGNESS**, all written by my good friend and co-creator, John Ira Thomas.

I live in a house in Iowa City with my wonderful partner of eleven years, David, and our two cats (Zazu & Noodles). John Ira lives in the basement.

We have CLP cookouts every Saturday throughout the summer… stop on by and have a beer with us!

Denise Sudell

www.sequentialtart.com

Denise Sudell is the Resident Lesbian (and a staff writer) at the award-winning, woman-produced comics webzine Sequential Tart. Her recent Tarticles about queers in comics include "Face-Off of the Flaming Queens," a comparison of Marvel's Rawhide Kid with DC Comics/Vertigo's Go-Go Fiasco and Donna Barr's Desert Peach.

Since mid-2002, she's been a member of the Comic Book Nominating Committee for the Gay and Lesbian Alliance Against Defamation (GLAAD)'s annual Media Awards.

She also hangs out on (and serves as Assistant Sysop for) the CompuServe Comics Forum, whose members have been described by the ever-charitable Warren Ellis as "fangeezers."

In her paying job, she's an attorney working underground (read: within the system) to keep the evil overseers of the Bush administration from dismantling U.S. federal civil rights laws.

Primary turn-on: sanity. Turn-offs include poor punctuation and Rick Santorum.

Rich Thigpen

rich@prismcomics.org

One of the writers of Prism Comics' popular **Queer Eye on Comics** weekly review series, Rich Thigpen also serves on the organization's Board of Directors as Membership Chair. A Los Angeles computer consultant by day, he also enjoys going to the gym, doing volunteer work (including granting wishes to seriously ill children through Starlight Starbright Children's Foundation), and playing with his cats.

Michael Troy

www.greencandypress.com

Michael Troy was born in the Midwest (don't hold that against him) in the seventies. He has been drawing since he picked up his first crayon—baby blue, his signature color.

Michael's goal in life is to become more whimsical and he thought a coloring book of naked superheroes would be a good place to start. Thus, **HOMO-HERO'S BIG BOOK OF FUN AND ADVENTURE** was born. Michael is hoping to make the Homo-hero an in-your-face non-ambiguously gay icon for proud gay men everywhere.

Michael now lives in Southern California where he performs stand-up comedy on a regular basis while also pursuing his acting and art careers. He is currently working on a new project called **THE BLONDE SQUAD**, which is about a team of shallow superheroes in Los Angeles.

Ivan Velez, Jr.

www.planetbronx.com

Raised in the South Bronx, Ivan was heavily influenced by the chop-socky karate flicks, **Astro Boy** cartoons, blaxploitation films, Spanish soap operas, and Silver Age comic books that filled every second of his free time. So far, that hasn't changed.

His work has been seen in several issues of **GAY COMICS**, *Details* magazine, *NYQ*, and *HX*. He has sold scripts to HBO and the Hudlin Brothers. He has also been reviewed in the *Advocate*, *Edge*, the *Village Voice*, the *New York Times* and on NPR.

Ivan has written several Milestone titles, including **BLOOD SYNDICATE** (which included character design for some of the cast), **A MAN CALLED HOLOCAUST**, and a year-long run on the acclaimed series **STATIC**. Both **BLOOD SYNDICATE** and **STATIC** won awards on his shift.

Ivan has also written for the mainstream, bless his little soul. He scripted a **VENOM** mini-series, the last two years on **GHOST RIDER**, and **ABOMINATIONS**, among others for Marvel. At DC Comics, he wrote the **ERADICATOR** mini-series, did some hard time on **EXTREME JUSTICE**, and a story for Vertigo's **FLINCH**. He continues to do the odd **POWERPUFF GIRLS** story at their kid division.

He has finished his first short film, *Malaguena* (a ghost story), and is writing his first novel, *Opaline's Secret*.

Ivan is mostly known as the creator of **TALES OF THE CLOSET**, a ten-chapter graphic novel that depicts the lives of eight gay teenagers in Queens. He has won a 2004 Xeric grant and will use this to begin publishing the series on his own imprint: Planet Bronx Productions.

Carlo Vergara

visprint.net/publications/zsazsa/index.html, www.gayleague.com/forums/display.php?id=376

Carlo loved to put lines together as a kid. He discovered that this was called "drawing." He drew and drew and drew, making comics in old notebooks.

After an attempt to create a comics series after college, he took to the corporate world and tried his hand in theater acting. But he wanted to make comics so much. So in 2001, he self-published **ONE NIGHT IN PURGATORY**, a short, slightly melodramatic tale about… well, two guys in love.

The following year, he turned to superhero comedy with **THE SPECTACULAR ADVENTURES OF ZSAZSA ZATURNNAH**, (title translated from Filipino) about a gay beautician who becomes a superhero. That graphic novel won a National Book Award from the Manila Critics Circle. In February 2006, Philippine theater company Tanghalang Pilipino will stage their musical adaptation of the graphic novel.

He just finished artwork for a story in the anthology **GRAPHIC CLASSICS: RAFAEL SABATINI**, which is scheduled for release also in February 2006. He's planning his next grafiction work while fulfilling his duties as an art director for a home decor and interior design magazine. He doesn't know spit about interior design, but he still likes to draw and draw and draw.

José Villarrubia

josevillar@aol.com

Born in Madrid, Spain, a long time Baltimore resident, and currently living in Paris, José Villarrubia is a painter/photographer/digital artist. His fine art photographs have been exhibited internationally and have been featured in the books *The Homoerotic Photograph*, *Lust: The Body Politic*, *The Male Nude, Uniforms: FotoFactory Anthology III*, and *Male Bonding: Volume Two*.

In comics he is best know for his painted/digital coloring in series such as **HELLSHOCK**, **THE SENTRY, FANTASTIC FOUR: 1 2 3 4, CAPTAIN AMERICA: RED, WHITE & BLUE, CAGE, XEN, THE BROTHERHOOD, CHAMBER, SUPERMAN: METROPOLIS, SPIDER-MAN-DOCTOR OCTOPUS: YEAR ONE**, and a myriad of covers including a run with Phil Jimenez in **WONDER WOMAN**.

His digital artwork was first seen in the Eisner-nominated Vertigo graphic novel **VEILS** in collaboration with Stephen John Phillips. His complete digital artwork made a splash in **PROMETHEA** #7, written by Alan Moore. He has also illustrated two books by Moore: a novel, *Voice Of The Fire* and an epic poem in prose, *The Mirror of Love,* both published by Top Shelf in 2003. *Mirror* is an important gay text that narrates the history of homosexuality and lesbianism in the form of a passionate love letter and a political manifesto. The book contains over 40 full-page color illustrations.

In 2002 his work was selected for the Society of Illustrators Annual Exhibition and he was nominated for an Eisner Award as Best Colorist.

This year he worked with Killian Plunkett in the **BATMAN BEGINS: THE MOVIE** ADAPTATION and the menu of the *Batman Begins DVD Special Edition*. He just completed **WOLVERINE #32** with Kaare Andrews and **BATMAN: GOTHAM COUNTY LINE** with Scott Hampton.

He is currently working with Paul Pope in **BATMAN: YEAR 100**, J. H. Williams in **DESOLATION JONES**, Ryan Sook in **X-FACTOR**, Jesus Sainz in **MANHUNTER** (covers), Chris Sprouse in **TOM STRONG #36**, Melinda Gebbie in **ABC, A to Z**, Kyle Hotz in **PUNISHER: SILENT #1**, and Michael Gaydos in **YOUNG AVENGERS SPECIAL**.

Taylor Vineyard

www.burntlatexproductions.com

Taylor Vineyard would die instantly if he could not draw. It's like oxygen to him-or so the legend goes.

The Portland, Oregon based illustrator and animator is the creator of **GIRINDA**, and the co-creator and artist for **GODLESS** as well as countless other illustrations over the past decade. A rare show of his early works and paintings from the **GIRINDA** back catalogue was a near sold-out event when it opened in November 2004.

He lives in Portland, with his partner, the writer and musician Andrew Klaus, two cats, and a dog in a rent-controlled apartment in a nice neighborhood that is rather questionable once the sun goes down.

Krista Ward

dreamhavenstudios@yahoo.com

Krista has been a colourist in the industry for over eight years now. She got her start at a studio called Heroic Age in 1997 and decided to venture out on her own in late 2003. She became the separator for the Marvel Comic series, **Thanos** in 2003 and continued until the title ended.

Krista has also worked on such titles as **HAWKMAN**, **JLA**, **JL ADVENTURES**, **ROBIN**, **TITANS**, **THE INFINITY ABYSS**, **THE END**, **THE NAIL**, **BATMAN: DARK VICTORY** and **THE LONG HALLOWEEN** and most recently, a **TRANSFORMERS** preview for the 2005 BotCon.

If you would like to contact her about colouring your project, please feel free to email her at the above address!

Kathryn Williams

www.katandnekomanga.ca

Most of Kathryn Williams' past is a blur of nightmarish images of pain and loss. Her first real memories are of laying in a hospital staring at the ceiling, unsure as to who she was or how she got where she was that day, but that didn't matter to her at all because she had nothing left to live for. No family, no friends and most of all she buried her first true love. The only thing that kept her from dying was a promise she made to her love that no matter what happened she would live on... for both of them.

She changed her last name as a sign that she wasn't going to look back at the person she used to be and look forward from then on. She struggled and fought her way back into school then finally graduated with a major in her second love, Arts. But something was still missing. So she again found herself staring at the ceiling again passing the time by drawing giant murals on her apartment walls. After a year of sitting around waiting for something to happen it finally did.

Attending an anime showing at a nearby university, she entered the club's mascot artist contest. The club liked the designs for what would become Neko Haruka, and she given the mascot job. Soon people were hounding her for more artwork.

With some newly found self-confidence Kathryn took the next impossible step. The World of Gallery arts. She did not expect the lack of respect in the art community for an artist who draws in the anime/manga style. Right when she was about to give up she was finally given a break when she was notified that her work would be put in the Gay Pride Art Show. People loved her work so much that Kathryn decided right then that this was what she was going to do. She was going to write about the one thing she knew about more then anything else. And she was going to publish it as a manga.

Kathryn quickly grew from an unknown artist to Guest of Honour at conventions around North America, and quickly gained the respect of many others in the industry, recognized as the only known North American Lesbian Shoujo Ai Mangaka. This, coupled with her journey to help other survivors through her stories, has lead to TV and newspaper interviews as well as numerous appearances at conventions. Now with the support of her fans she has begun to rewrite her first manga, A SHADOWLANDER'S DREAM, as well as print a new story told from the eyes of a rape survivor.

Now known simply as "Kat" she works long side the AniLesboCon in an effort to help bring the world of Shoujo Ai to others by helping with everything from creating a collective manga anthology to working on animation.

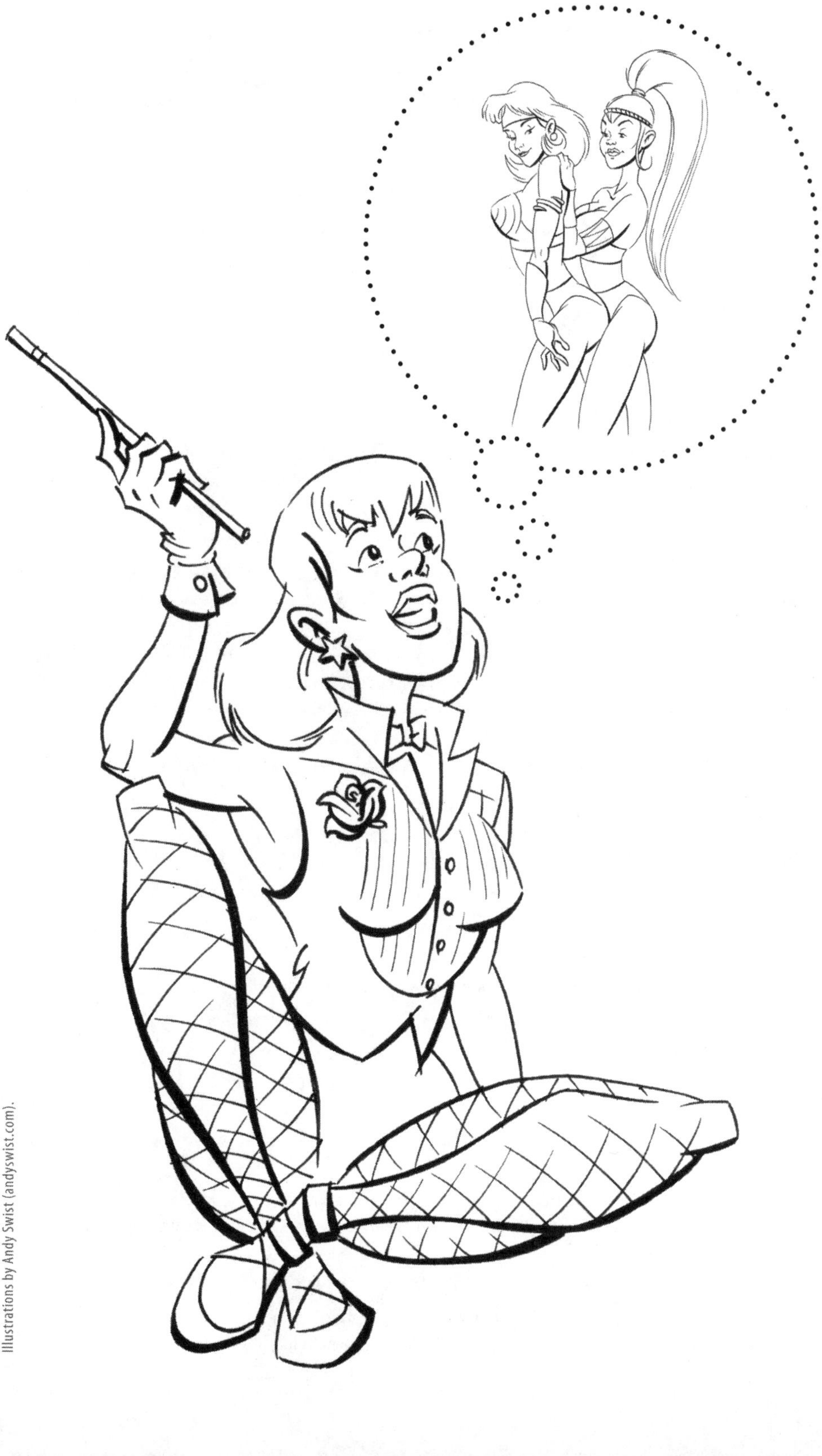

Illustrations by Andy Swist (andyswist.com).

resources

ALTERWORLDS
The Gay and Lesbian
Roleplaying Association

www.alterworlds.com

AlterWorlds is an online resource for gay and lesbian roleplaying gamers of all stripes. Currently, the site features an extensive member database (searchable by location) so you can find other "gay-mers" in your area to connect with. More resources are planned in the future.

ATDNSIN

www.northstar-atdnsin.com

(The APA That Dare Not Speak Its Name)

ATDNSIN, an Amateur Publishing Association (APA) for lesbians, gays, bisexuals & transgendered people, was begun in response to the 1989 San Diego Comic Con "Gays in Comics" panel. The APA has discussions on comics of all genres, how they relate to queer people, and the varied lifestyles.

Amateurs and professionals have interacted over the years, sending in their individual 'zine sections which may have art, cartoons, stories or personal discussion to the Central Mailer who collates the sections and sends the completed magazine to members. ATDNSIN contains adult content; you must be of legal age to join.

For a sample issue please send $5.00 to: Mike Phillips, Central Mailer, 1032 Irving Street, PMB - 614, San Francisco, CA 94122-2200

THE GAY COMICS LIST

http://gaycomicslist.free.frp

An excellent resources from François Peneaud, with lots of reviews of gay-themed comics, a gallery of "The Male Body in Comic Book Art" and other goodies.

THE GAY LEAGUE

www.gayleague.com

(or GLA) is an online federation of queer comics fans from all over the world. The GLA website contains information on gay characters, storylines and creators in comics. It's also home to a lively group who interact and share art, reviews, and stories.

GLA Yahoo Group

A great deal of the GLA members' interaction takes place via its e-mail lists at Yahoo! Groups. The regular list, called simply the GLA, is a great way to get to know other gay fans through the lively e-mail discussions they hold.

GLAFILES2 Yahoo Group

The GLAFiles2 is a companion list for members to share photos, drawings and more discussion. Due to some adult content, you must be of legal age in your locality to join the GLAFiles2.

GAYS & COMICS FORUM AT DELPHI

forums.delphiforums.com/gaycomics

A comics forum for queer comics fans and their straight sympathizer friends! The moderators of this forum are Andrew Wheeler and Christopher Butcher. They are warm, caring people who will take you down if you misbehave.

HOMNI: Comics

www.geocities.com/homni_ca/comics

A massive listing of queer material in comics, with lists of gay characters, creators, online cartoons and comics and a quick-jump menu that takes you to queer comics sites online.

Northstar

www.northstar-atdnsin.com

NORTHSTAR is the nation's fastest growing APA for LGBT comics fans, and was founded in 1989. Members submit self-made 'zines on comics and popular culture to the Central Mailer, who distributes the collected issue to the members. Nominal membership fees cover the cost of postage. NORTHSTAR celebrated its 50th Anniversary Issue in January of 2000.

'Zines often include stories, art, reviews, discussion, adult content, and provide a depth of personality that is hard to find online. Sharing creative juices and building lasting friendships are the focus.

For a sample issue please send $5.00 to: Mike Phillips, Central Mailer, 1032 Irving Street, PMB - 614, San Francisco, CA 94122-2200

OUTWORLDERS

www.outworlders.info

Outworlders is a science fiction, fantasy, and horror fan group that supports and promotes gay, lesbian, bisexual and transgender themes within these genres. Everyone is welcome. An interest in the genres and an open mind are the only requirements. Our members are as diverse as their interests, and enjoy exploring fandom in a welcoming community of like minded people.

QueerNet

groups.queernet.org

Founded in 1996, the queercomix mailing list has been a discussion area and "safe space" on the Internet for talk about queer issues in comic books. Anything directly relating to queer concerns in comic books and the comics industry is appropriate for discussion, including in-story and personnel issues. Queer characters, creators, storylines and themes, and even queer-phobic creators, publishers, and/or comic book stories are all discussed regularly by the members. The queercomix list is not a general-purpose "home base" for queer fans to discuss anything comics related (or even unrelated) — it has a narrower focus, and off-topic discussions are not encouraged.

COMICNURSE.COM

NOT DONE YET

The true story of
Little Miss Muffet
by Lynx Delirium

Fairies Tail

carabossecomics.com

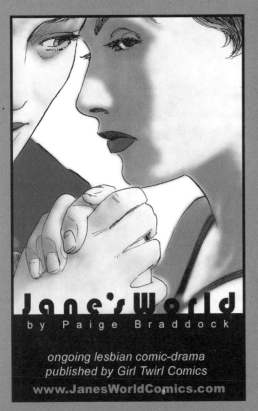

Jane's World
by Paige Braddock

*ongoing lesbian comic-drama
published by Girl Twirl Comics*

www.JanesWorldComics.com

BENEFACTORS

Prism Comics is proud to thank the people who have supported us in the past year. As an all-volunteer organization, we depend on community contributions to do our work. With you, we work toward our goal of a more diverse comics industry and promote great comics that deserve wider recognition.

Thanks to our donors and volunteers, we've not only been able to take on large projects like providing creators and fans booth space at conventions, but also smaller ones like mailing our guides to members of the press and keeping our feature-rich Web-site current and exciting.

Every gift is important and appreciated, whether it's original artwork, comics to stock our convention booths and online store or a monetary donation. Please support Prism Comics today to further build on our successes in advancing the awareness of the gay community in comics. You can visit our website at www.prismcomics.org and make a donation quickly and easily.

Thank you!
The Volunteers at Prism Comics

this year and in the past

Mara Baz	David Krantz
Alison Bechdel	LA Pride
Gary Beck	Doug Lawrence
Paige Braddock	Norman Franklin
Leland Burrill	Lloyd
Can-Am Video	James Locke
David Carter	Michael Lovitz
Charles "zan"	Edward Matthews
Christensen	Marco Magana
Vinnie Costa	François Peneaud
Dark Horse	PKA
Comics	Brad Rader
Peter Di Maso	Milton Rodriguez
Neil Gaiman	Stephen Sadowski
Victor Hodge	Greg Sanchez
Image Comics	Jeffrey Sass
Patty Jeres	Sean-Z
Phil Jimenez	David Stanley
Ross Katz	Donald Steffen
Anton Kawasaki	Rich Thigpen
Chip Kidd	TokyoPop
Todd Killinger	Elizabeth Watasin
Robert Kirby	David Welsh
Roger Klorese	Joe Zilvinskis